Reinventure

How Travel Adventures
Can Change Your Life

Carol Patterson

Order this book online at www.trafford.com/08-0116
or email orders@trafford.com

Most Trafford titles are also available at major online book retailers.

Note for Librarians: A cataloguing record for this book is available from Library
and Archives Canada at www.collectionscanada.ca/amicus/index-e.html

Printed in Victoria, BC, Canada.

ISBN: 978-1-4251-6979-4

*We at Trafford believe that it is the responsibility of us all, as both individuals
and corporations, to make choices that are environmentally and socially sound.
You, in turn, are supporting this responsible conduct each time you purchase a
Trafford book, or make use of our publishing services. To find out how you are
helping, please visit www.trafford.com/responsiblepublishing.html*

*Our mission is to efficiently provide the world's finest, most comprehensive
book publishing service, enabling every author to experience success.
To find out how to publish your book, your way, and have it available
worldwide, visit us online at www.trafford.com/10510*

 www.trafford.com

North America & international
toll-free: 1 888 232 4444 (USA & Canada)
phone: 250 383 6864 ♦ fax: 250 383 6804 ♦ email: info@trafford.com

The United Kingdom & Europe
phone: +44 (0)1865 487 395   local rate: 0845 230 9601
facsimile: +44 (0)1865 481 507   mail: info.uk@trafford.com

10 9 8 7 6 5 4 3

For Colin
whose wisdom and joyfulness inspires me

Acknowledgements

"Vision without action is hallucination." ~ *Don Clinton*

A book concept without a support network can cause hallucinations. In following my vision, I owe a debt of gratitude to those who have sustained me. First and foremost is Don Morberg, my editor and mentor. Don is a gifted writer in his own right, and has generously shared his insights, editing magic, and design concepts. I could not have done it without you!

From the earliest days of Kalahari Management, Shelley McReynolds has cheered me on and suggested this book of tales. Hope Bishop has provided honest feedback when I needed it most and bravely accompanied me on several travel adventures. My husband, Colin has ferried me to the airport more times than I can count, and listens to my tales of woe and wonder.

Thanks to John Hull, Albert Teo, and Bob Garrison for making the tourism projects in my stories so memorable and enjoyable.

Kudos to the people who shared their stories for the book; research was never so much fun! Dave Elston, your cartoons capture travel in a way words never could.

I'm grateful to Brian Keating of the Calgary Zoo for approving my crazy idea for a Flying Zoo so many years ago, and for accelerating my interest in wildlife. The Calgary Zoo and its dedicated staff have been my inspiration.

My belief that Reinventure transcends backgrounds and age has been strengthened by my nephews Adam, Cody, Erik, Evan and Jared. Their willingness to bug watch through the 'wrong' end of the binoculars proves all creatures can create glee.

Although there are too many to name, I am inspired by the dedication, sacrifice and perseverance of the many professionals, business owners, and community volunteers I've met in the field of nature tourism. They share my vision of a better world from travel done responsibly.

To all my friends, family and supporters, thank you for being part of my amazing journey! May all your Reinventures be rewarding!

Carol

Table of Contents

Introduction

It's early Tuesday morning, summer 1992, and I'm not at my desk. I'm not wearing a business suit and heels. I'm not entering numbers into spreadsheets. I'm wearing my hiking boots and I'm crouched low on the side of a mountain road watching a helicopter fly in to pick me up. I close my eyes against the dust whipped up by its rotor blades. Today I'm not an accountant. Today I'm an ecotourism consultant. How did this happen?

I suddenly realize that my love of the outdoors, wildlife and adventure has taken me out of the office and into a new and exciting career. I realize my life has undergone the change that I'd hoped for, but feared might not happen.

There had been hints earlier in my life that my career might not look like the standard occupations in a guidance counselor's check-off list like nurse, teacher or police officer.

One of my favorite childhood games was pretending I was a famous animal trainer. I convinced my siblings and playmates to be lions, dogs and whales. The backyard was transformed to a zoo or aquarium, the latter requiring real imagination since I grew up in the short grass prairies of western Canada.

When I was ten, I created my first wildlife attraction. I collected dozens and dozens of lady bugs, placing them in a bucket with what I thought was a suitable habitat – lots of leaves, rocks and twigs to climb on. I was crushed a few hours later when I found the bucket overturned and my collection gone, the bugs having fled back to the garden. I was to learn much later that keeping real life tourism attractions going was just as hard!

At sixteen, I decided I would become a park ranger. I raced home from school with the college catalogue, exhilarated by the idea of working with animals and wearing a real park ranger's uniform. My mother gave me a quick reality check. She pointed out that I didn't like bugs (ladybugs were the exception), that I got cold easily in the outdoors, and that living in remote locations would be tough for a woman. I had to concede she had more than a few valid points so I went with a more logical choice and became an accountant. There was always work for accountants even if I dreaded the idea of routine days.

When I moved to Calgary in 1980 to do accounting work for an energy company, my inner park ranger came back to life. I discovered the Calgary Zoo and soon became a devoted visitor. I couldn't get enough during regular visits so I became a volunteer, first as a docent leading tours of the Zoo, then as a member of the Zoo's education committee. I wanted to learn more about the zoo's operations and moved on to become a trustee on the board of directors. I chaired the Live Collections and Business Operations committees and ultimately became Chairman of the Board of Directors. As I was moving through those roles, I discovered the Zoo's ecotourism program.

In 1985, the Zoo offered a trip to Namibia, Botswana and South Africa jammed with wildlife watching opportunities and led by the Zoo's Head of Conservation Outreach Brian Keating. It was an irresistible opportunity and I signed on (although with a great deal of trepidation.) I'd just purchased my first house and money was tight, but I figured this was the kind of trip a person should do when they are young. I went for it! When the plane touched down at Johannesburg airport, I felt like I was coming home even though I'd never before set foot in Africa. Seeing my first wild animal, an elegant impala near Namibia's Etosha Pans, started me on a picture-taking frenzy and sent shivers up my spine.

My parents saw no reason for an accountant to run off to Africa. I told them this safari was an exotic adventure to take before I "settled down." To my parent's chagrin, the first safari led to another and another. I was fascinated at seeing the wildlife I'd only read about as a child. Furthermore, I was enchanted by the idea that travel could help these animals. Ironically, habitat land is scarce in Africa and I quickly recognized that tourism provided the economic justification to keep vital wildlife land out of agricultural or industrial development.

I soon realized there had to be a way for me to make a living by combining business with wildlife conservation and travel. I was determined to find it. As I waited on the side of the road for the helicopter that would take me into a remote mountain lodge, I realized that travel had taken me literally and figuratively to a world I preferred.

I scrambled in beside the pilot and we took off. Within seconds I had a mind-popping view of the Rocky Mountains. The 20 minute trip gave me a chance to see above the valley bottoms to the hidden glaciers and back canyons that hikers rarely see. We landed in a lush alpine meadow surrounded by towering peaks, naked of snow in the weeks before the fall precipitation started.

Don, the lodge owner, greeted me with a friendly handshake and took me on a tour of his camp. The main lodge was old and squat; its heavy wood beams and small windows lacked the glitz of modern hotels but they bespoke of its ability to withstand fierce summer storms and winter blizzards. The inside of the Lodge was decorated in Rocky Mountain rustic with some interesting keepsakes, conversation pieces for hikers after a day on the trails.

A short walk out the front door was a small, crystal clear lake. It was easy to imagine visitors sitting on the grassy banks watching the clouds chasing across the sky and letting the hours slip by. I was there to assess his business plans for the lodge and for the people he hoped to bring to this valley, but I was struck by his passion for the mountains and his desire to share it with travellers.

In the years since that day, I've met lots of people with a passion for travel. Many of them spend all their spare dollars and time on it. Some have given up well-paying jobs or prosperous businesses to create a career and life in tourism. Their lifestyles and backgrounds are as varied as the colors in a rainbow and just as fascinating to watch.

I realized that day in 1992 that travel had changed my life and eventually I came to realize that it has changed the lives of other people as well. I've come across hundreds of stories of how travel has transformed people and the communities where they live; so I decided to record some of them. Not all the stories are earth-shattering epiphanies; some are just gentle adjustments. Not everyone's story is uplifting either. Each of us can probably recall at least one travel horror that makes great retelling.

This book is a celebration of travel. I've felt its positive effects and I've seen it change others. Hopefully you'll see yourself in some of the adventures, and be inspired to create your own Reinventure!

Section One – Experiences

"Experience is what you get when you don't get what you want." ~ *Dan Stanford*

The Llama Legend, *page 18*

If you're the first person on your block to climb Mt. Everest, you can count on being the centre of attention at next year's neighborhood Christmas party. It seems that more and more we measure our success by the experiences we've had. In their best-selling book, *The Experience Economy,* Joseph Pine and James Gilmour tell business owners how to make more profits by creating and selling experiences rather than goods or services. Francis Farrell, publisher of National Geographic Travel magazine, goes so far as to call experiences "our new currency."

As I learned from talking to travellers and travel professionals, sometimes the best trips were the ones that had the most unexpected experiences. People said they remembered these trips or they enjoyed them the most because they had a chance to test their survival skills or strength of character. It is easy to be cheerful when everything is going well; but smiling when your flight is canceled or when there are no rooms at the inn, takes a bit more effort.

In this group of stories I share some of the unusual situations I and other travellers have encountered. As a tourism insider, I often get 'behind the scenes' views of travel destinations or attractions. The appeal of learning more about the fascinating world of travel never fades for me. I hope you enjoy a look past the glossy tourism advertisements to the daily reality for those of us with travel in our blood.

Who Let The Dogs Out?

"The World is a book, and those who do not travel read only a page."
~ Saint Augustine

One of the things I love most about my work in tourism planning is that I am often invited to speak at tourism conferences. I get the chance to meet some wonderful people and sample some of the unique experiences their community offers. In 2002, I was speaking at a conference in Sudbury, a nickel-mining town in Northern Ontario now working to develop a nature-based tourism industry. The conference was held in February and I was looking forward to the field trips because dog sledding was one of our choices. I jumped at the chance to sign up.

After putting on the half dozen layers I knew I'd need to stay warm (Mom really had been right when she said I got too cold for regular outdoor work) I was ready to go. Our little group tripped off the shuttle bus to meet Tom, the owner of the kennel, and his noisy and enthusiastic sled dogs.

We got the usual safety briefing about riding in the basket and keeping our hands inside so we didn't lose any digits. Eventually it dawned on me that Tom was giving us a lot of detail for riding in a dogsled. I mean, did we really need to remember the difference between gee and haw (the commands for turning left and right) if we were just to sit in the sled and admire the scenery? Then it became clear that Tom intended us to drive the dogsleds!

From my limited knowledge of dogsledding, 'driving' a dogsled was perhaps an optimistic interpretation of the experience. Once the dogs were hooked up to the sled, only a firm attachment to a nearby fence kept the dogs from leaving without us, command or no command. When you want to stop, you throw out a large hook, like a ship at sea. Not exactly precision controls, especially if the anchor doesn't catch. And the success of the left and right commands depends entirely on the training and hearing levels and inclination of the lead dogs. Any breakdown in that communication and you could find yourself wrapped around parts of the boreal forest.

Each sled in our caravan of five had three passengers and six dogs. The plan was to follow Tom, one team behind another, out of the parking lot and onto a small lake. Tom assured us we'd be safe; a frozen lake has few obstacles. That's a real bonus when you're a neophyte musher. My sled team included myself, two other women and a team of energetic, barking dogs. One person would ride in the basket and the other two would ride on the back struts of the sled, pushing when we came to hills.

Tom said our most important job would be to keep an eye on our dogs and make sure none of them were having problems. He explained that the dogs' natural instinct would be to follow the sled ahead of them so steering wouldn't take up too much of our time.

I was the first person to ride in the basket and it was a total thrill when we were unhooked from the fence and the dogs bolted down the trail. The ride was a bit bumpier than your average Cadillac, but a lot more fun. For a few short minutes, everything went smoothly, but then I noticed one of our dogs sitting down on the job as we were whipping across the lake. The poor canine had to be getting a snow enema, judging by the speed we were moving.

Fortunately, Tom chose that moment to stop and check on his teams. I ran up to him to explain about our dog that wouldn't run.

"He's a young dog," Tom explained, "Unhook his back harness connection so he doesn't feel claustrophobic and he should run fine." That sounded like a reasonable explanation so I sprinted back to unhook the dog and we set off again.

At first everything went as planned; all the dogs running and the sound of the sled swooshing over the snow lulling us into a state of euphoria. Before long, the young dog had sat down and was again being pulled by his teammates. Tom stopped again and I ran up to tell him the dog still wasn't pulling. Tom had some surprising advice, "Unhook the dog totally from the harness," he said.

"Won't he run away?" I asked.

"Nope," Tom said, "They are pack animals and he won't want to leave his friends." Well, Tom knows his dogs so we'll do it his way. I unhooked the dog from the harness and we started again.

Our free dog ran alongside the rest of our team with his tongue lolling out the side of his mouth, almost smiling with the joy of running with the pack without having to do any of the hard work. If word gets out about this, I thought, we're going to have a problem. Sure enough within a few minutes, we had a second dog sitting down on the job and being pulled by the team. Tom was now stopping every few minutes, so I ran up to tell him about the latest dog that had stopped pulling.

He repeated his advice to unhook the back harness. We did that and got a few more minutes of traction before the dog sat down again and let the team pull him along the snow. By now, I was getting as much exercise as the dogs with my runs up to Tom and back in my Michelin-man garb.

I wasn't surprised when Tom told me to unhook the dog totally from harness and let him run beside the sled. Now we were down to four dogs and I was hoping they were all middle-age dogs with no sense of claustrophobia or we were going to be calling a tow truck for our sled.

With only one more dog than passengers, we had to help the team by pushing off with one leg as we hung onto the sled's back supports. This 'pedaling' uses up a large amount of energy and I could see why no dog musher is ever seen with a Spa Lady membership. I gave my spot in the basket to one of the girls who was tiring out and took my turn pedaling.

My legs were turning to rubber as we made the push for home and the end of the lake. A sharp turn was the only remaining obstacle before the parking lot and the hot chocolate. I yelled out 'Haw' with what little oxygen remained in my lungs and watched in horror as the team didn't turn in time, but continued over the road and into the trees. I guess we had been left with hard working but hard-of-hearing dogs. Fortunately, by this time we weren't moving at any great speed, and only the first two dogs had gone into the bushes before the team came to a stop. I jumped off and ran up to show the dogs what a left turn looked like.

As I hopped back on for the short run to the end of the trail, I found myself chuckling. It occurred to me that most community

tourism projects are a lot like dog sledding. In every community
there are a handful of people who do the heavy lifting, helping
on projects from soup to nuts, while a few run alongside the
team enjoying the view and taking the reflected credit without
doing a share of the pulling. I can use that lesson in my
presentations!

Reptile Search And Rescue

*"If God had really intended men to fly, he'd make it easier to get to the
airport."* ~ George Winters

Before I officially joined the travel industry as a consultant,
I looked for every opportunity for adventure. I'd always been
fascinated by flying and in 1983 I took the money I'd made
working as an accountant in the far north and signed up for
flying lessons. I learned proper pre-flight inspection, touch and
go landings and how to decipher the garbled instructions from
the control tower. After conquering my fear of solo spins, I was
the proud holder of a private pilot's license.

Flying isn't cheap and I soon discovered that my budget and
spare time limited my trips to 60 minutes sorties around
Calgary. I like the challenge of trying new things so I came
up with what I thought was the inspired idea of combining my
flying skills with my docent duties at the Calgary Zoo. There
are kids living in rural communities around Calgary that do
not get to visit the zoo very often. Perhaps I could fly some
of the zoo's ambassador animals to these communities and do
interpretative programs on environmental topics.

It took a pitcher of margaritas to convince the Zoo's Education
Manager, Brian Keating that this would be a good project.
He got approval from the Board and some donations to cover
the cost of fuel. Several zookeepers suggested animals I could
take on the road. The Zoo already had a program called Zoo
to You where docents took small animals to senior's centers
and schools. This would be similar except we would fly, so

the program became known as the Calgary Zoo's Flying Zoo To You.

A Cessna 172 we rented from the local Flying Club isn't a big plane. Taking another docent, I was limited to animals that were small enough and light enough to fit into the plane's backseat without putting us over the weight limit.

The biggest animal I took on the program was Sarah, a Malaysian Binturong. Most people have never seen these creatures, but they are best described as a cross between a bear and a cat. Sarah was about the size and weight of a German shepherd. Occasionally, she would get a bit airsick, but overall she was a great passenger and extremely popular with the kids.

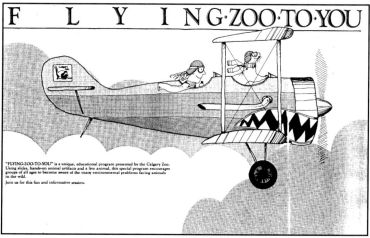

Poster advertising the upcoming arrival of Carol Patterson and her airborne Calgary Zoo animals.

For other trips I took a baby porcupine, small owls, snakes and lizards. The birds were nervous fliers; probably figuring they were the better aviators. I liked to travel with the reptiles, especially the snakes, because they do not have inner ears and never got airsick. I also didn't need to carry food for them as they could go weeks without a meal. My only problem was getting the flying club administrator to convince other pilots that I had accounted for all the snakes when I brought the plane back. I had 'Snakes On A Plane' years before the hit movie came out.

On one particularly memorable trip, I was very glad though to be travelling with reptiles. I was doing a trip to Bassano, a small community an hour and half drive from Calgary, but only a few minutes by plane. Under sunny skies, a friendly welcoming committee of local residents met the plane and whisked us off to the library for our talk.

By the time I had finished up the interpretive program, the weather had turned stormy. Pat, the other docent, and I went out to the airstrip, but a look at the skies had me worried about getting home. I was only rated for visual flying rules (VFR), I couldn't fly through clouds. I quickly called the flying club for an updated forecast and had my fears confirmed. We would have to wait for the thunderstorms to pass.

Pat and I headed off the local hotel for some comfort food; nothing soothes nerves in a crisis like fries and gravy! We spent the afternoon slurping pop and sharing stories while Rosie, the two-metre boa constrictor, and the skink rested in their travelling crates. As the day slipped away, it was clear we were not going to get the kind of skies we needed to fly home. I checked the bus schedules and saw that there would be a bus bound for Calgary at 4 p.m.

I called Brian, the chief pilot, to tell him we would have to leave the plane and come back for it another day. He was horrified; not about the plane but about the animals. "How are you going to get a snake and a lizard on the bus?" he asked.

"I'm going to tell them it's beer," I replied. The Styrofoam travelling cases looked a lot like picnic coolers, "Everyone takes beer on the bus!"

He took a minute to mull that thought over and to talk to another flying instructor. Soon he was back with a better plan.

"It's a slow day what with the storms and everything. We're going to fly over and ferry you back," he said. I figured the Zoo and I would both be happier with that solution, so our hosts loaded us into their van and we headed yet again to the airstrip.

Within minutes a Cessna appeared out of the clouds, and landed near our plane. Brian took the co-pilot's seat on my plane and we took off for Calgary, zigzagging around the clouds. By this time, we were overdue on our flight plan and the Zoo was short two animals from its collection. A quick explanation over the radio (sometimes truth is stranger than fiction) set everything straight.

We were back at the Calgary airport in minutes offloading the snake and the lizard. Brian watched, making sure his least favorite reptile didn't get left behind by mistake. With a sigh of relief, I turned over the snake and lizard at the Zoo gates. I'm pretty sure the flying club made history that day with the first ever reptile search and rescue.

Flying In The Day

"The saying 'Getting there is half the fun' became obsolete with the advent of commercial airlines." ~ Henry J. Tillman

In addition to giving me some great memories with the Flying Zoo To You program, my pilot's license has provided me other memorable experiences when I was travelling. One of the great bonuses of being an aviator has been the many invitations to visit the cockpits of the commercial aircraft I've travelled in. Of course 9/11 changed all that, but passing the time on long flights was a lot easier when there was a chance to see out the front window.

My first trip to Africa required a South African Airlines flight from New York City via Johannesburg, South Africa, to Namibia and Botswana. It was the height of apartheid riots and our trip organizers had many discussions with the Canadian Consulate on whether it was safe to go. Even though we were only staying overnight in South Africa, we were worried if we would be safe or not.

Apparently more than a few other people had those some concerns and our flight from New York City to Johannesburg was nearly empty. Most people were giddy with the thought of a whole row of airplane seats to stretch out on, but I was almost beside myself with excitement when I found out the tour leader, himself a private pilot, had finagled an invite into the cockpit once we were at cruising altitude. After the in-flight meal, people snuggled down for some shut eye with a full belly. With the interior lights down low, the plane was quiet as we made our way up the aisle.

The pilot and co-pilots welcomed us into the cockpit and patiently answered our questions about the big bird. I will never forget the hour or so that we spent crouched on the floor watching the night sky as the plane zipped across the Atlantic Ocean at 37,000 feet. It was one of those special moments where you realize you're experiencing something so rare few people including yourself will ever repeat it.

I was doubly lucky on that trip because in Namibia I was able to garner another once-in-a-lifetime flying experience. After game viewing one afternoon in Etosha National Park, I met a young South African pilot, Paul, who was there to fly some photographers around the park. Paul invited me to join the flight they had planned for that evening over the salt pans. Not wanting to miss perhaps my one and only chance to fly in a King Air I eagerly accepted. Paul introduced me as his co-pilot to the group of photographers and gave me the right hand seat. Given my meager number of flying hours in a Cessna, I figured the copilot label was a bit of a stretch, but I didn't have to do anything except smile and accept the perks.

I found out fast that King Airs can do things a small Cessna cannot. We taxied to the end of the runway and took off in a climb so steep the stall indicator started screaming and never stopped. Not something that was recommended in my flight training, as I recall. I might have been concerned, but Paul looked like he had a healthy self-preservation instinct, so I sat back to enjoy the ride.

The sun was low in the sky and the colors so rich and vivid it made me wish I was a painter so I could capture them properly. Paul swooped the plane higher in the sky and then we darted low back and forth over the pan in series of aerial maneuvers I could only marvel at. The photographers were treated to incredible views of the African landscape and the zebra, ostrich and elephant that dotted it. A couple of the shutterbugs rolled into the aisle when caught unawares by the rapid change in the direction, but there were no complaints. We were all enjoying the show.

We touched down as the sun was setting and, after a short taxi, parked the plane. Etosha National Park travel rules state that all vehicles must be off the roads by sunset; and the gates to the camps locked. Despite racing back to camp in our truck, we found the camp gates were locked.

Paul must have been a Boy Scout when younger, he was prepared. He had invited one of the park rangers along as a guest on our flight. While we sat on the road outside the gate, the park ranger jumped out and whistled. Less than a minute later, the gates swung open and we were on our way to the bar to relive our adventures and cement new friendships.

Into The Bridge

"We wander for distraction, but we travel for fulfillment." ~ *Hilaire Belloc*

My flying these days is done in the back of a commercial aircraft as I journey to consulting projects or to speak at conferences. Sadly, flying has become the inconvenience between home and work, but I can still count on a fair amount of excitement at the other end when I do site visits to attractions and tourism facilities to determine how best to improve the region's prospects.

As a tourism professional, I'm often invited to see new attractions and meet with the managers to learn how they have succeeded in building or marketing their facilities. The conference organizers of the 2007 Travel Tourism and Research Association came up with one of the most unusual experiences I've seen.

"We're going into the bridge," our host exclaimed. I thought I had misheard. "Into?"

When I had signed up for the case study tour, I knew we would be visiting the Confederation Bridge, a 12.9 kilometre (eight mile) link between Canada's Prince Edward Island and the New Brunswick coastline. The Travel Tourism and Research Association prides itself on sharing the latest tourism research at its annual conference, and since the event was being held in PEI, a visit to the bridge seemed a logical add-on. Ten years had passed since the once highly-controversial bridge had opened. We would hear how its presence had impacted tourism and the island way of life.

We stopped at a small theatre in the picturesque village of Victoria-by-the-sea to meet a representative from Tourism PEI. He told us the number of visitors had increased by almost 50 per cent since the bridge had opened, but the island way of life was not being negatively impacted. In fact the opposite was true. Better access to the rest of Canada has made it easier to conduct business and keep appointments off the island.

"Some winter days you would spend almost twenty hours on the ferry as it tried to work its way through the ice. It would go back and forth across the channel trying to find a way through the ice; sometimes it was painfully slow. Now we can drive across the bridge in fifteen minutes regardless of the ice," he said.

The media had given the bridge a lot of attention when it was first built. It was the longest free standing single span bridge in the world, built to withstand the pressure of winter ice pushing against its pillars. It cost an astounding $ 1 billion to build, to be paid for over many years by bridge tolls.

So when our host for the day said "You're in for something special", I thought we were going to get a narrated drive across the bridge. But I had heard right, we were getting the extremely rare opportunity to go inside the bridge! I didn't realize bridges had insides, but this one does. The salt water and strong winds would make maintenance difficult if there wasn't a contained area for the electrical systems and service staff.

The engineer, our tour guide for the afternoon, outfitted us with spiffy hard hats but no one complained about hat hair.

"The inside corridor isn't meant for tourists so you need to watch for hazards when you are walking," our guide said. "There are sharp wires sticking out of the electrical panel at eye level so be very careful." My Mom always warned us we would poke an eye out if we horsed around with sharp objects. I realized I'd been training for this tour my whole life!

Like school kids, we lined up at the door to the bridge, eager to head into the bowels. We were to walk a kilometre out of over the Atlantic Ocean and time was tight, so we'd have to hurry.

Normally I'm not much interested in bricks and mortar when I'm sightseeing, but being inside this huge bridge was pretty cool, literally and figuratively. The corridor was completely made of cement with no windows. It was dark and damp and it smelled a little bit like someone's unfinished basement. As we started our walk along the bridge floor, I felt like a character in a Disney cartoon. Instead of walking over a horizontal surface we were following the curves of the bridge structure; walking up to the top of upside-down 'U' and then down the other side. Lights lit up the junctures between the arches and our group marched towards the light like moths to a flame. Then we'd leave that juncture and walk into the darkness over the next arch.

The further we walked the more dramatic the inclines became and then we started to get glimpses of the ocean below. Small holes every few hundred metres gave us a bird's eye view of the water and a reminder that we were at thirty metres above the sea. The engineer explained that the bridge is really three bridges in one. The sections that link to land on both sides are built like traditional bridges. The long centre portion is a suspension bridge. We were able to see the contraction joints that allow the cement to expand and contract with the weather.

Some people wanted to walk the length of the bridge into New Brunswick. That would be a tale to tell, but all too soon it was time to turn around. As we retraced our steps, I realized how rare such an experience was in our post 9/11 world. Security concerns mean that behind-the-scenes tours of bridges, plants and airports are no longer an option. I was secretly thrilled to have had the experience, and a little less than proud to realize part of the enjoyment I felt was knowing that it was a very unique experience few others will enjoy. If there were bridge tours departing every hour, I doubt I would have spared the time to take it. I guess in a lot of ways we are all still childlike in our behavior. Tell us we can't do something and we will be giddy when we manage to do it. Give us free will to do something and it loses its appeal. There is a lesson there.

The Llama Legend

"Travel is only glamorous in retrospect." ~ Paul Theroux

One of the reasons I got into the travel business was that I wanted other people to find the same pleasure in nature I enjoy while travelling. Usually most trips are pleasant with no major incidents. Occasionally luggage goes lost or traveller's diarrhea hits someone unlucky enough to eat bad Mexican food, but most people take their holidays and come back with nothing but great memories. Such was not the case with a group of women I took llama trekking. Afterwards they were congratulating themselves on just surviving the experience.

The trip had started with great promise. A group of old friends were looking for a chance to break away from the responsibilities of being wives, mothers, professionals, etc. and become cocky, wild-eyed adventurers for a short time. I found a company that offered overnight llama trekking trips in the mountains and decided it was a great way to spend a girl's weekend. The llamas would do the hard work; carrying our gear up the mountains and we'd be free to hike unencumbered, chatting and admiring the mountain scenery. I called the company and made the arrangements for our group.

Right off, there were warning signs that things would not go as planned. A weather forecast predicted snow at higher elevations, but Cheryl, our tour operator, said it was unlikely the warm September weather would turn that cold on our route. One of the women pulled out of the trip with health concerns. We felt bad that she had to forfeit her entire trip payment; by the end of the weekend she looked like a psychic genius. All of us would have willingly paid several times the trip cost to be airlifted out of the mountains half way through the trip.

The morning dawned clear and bright as so many of these 'experiences' often do. We met Cheryl and her furry army of llamas at the staging area. There was a llama for each. My llama, Zeke, was a handsome creature and looked sturdy enough to carry a large load; but peered down his nose at me with studied indifference. More than once, I could have sworn his expression said "You expect me to do what?"

Eventually we set off down the trail, our llamas bobbing gently alongside. They are so light on their feet that it felt a bit like pulling a balloon on a string.

We had been warned that we would have to do several river crossings and had come prepared with extra shoes. The cold water was a shock as it rose almost to my knees. In short order I could barely feel my feet, but rather than dash across the river as was my first inclination, I had to pick my way slowly across the river at Zeke speed. His river boots were fur lined and he wasn't in any big rush. It didn't get easier with each river crossing. Our shoes were now thoroughly wet; our feet stayed cold and the weather turned cloudy and cool.

Most people who live or play in the mountains know the weather can change quickly and we got a first-hand demonstration after lunch. The cool rain we had been hiking in for an hour turned to snow. These weren't the little flakes that look a lot like rain, these were the big, fat ones that pile up in a hurry.

Cheryl hurried across one more river crossing then told us to set up camp before the snow obscured the ground. We pitched tents at a speed that would have made a Boy Scout proud. Unfortunately the Boy Scouts come prepared. We had three-season tents; definitely not built for snow. Before we could get in them for shelter, they started to collapse under the weight of the snowstorm. We looked for tree wells that would give us shelter and dragged the tents to the largest of these. There wasn't enough room to be comfortable, but if we were to avoid serious trouble we were going to have to make do. Hope and Cherry stuffed their tent into the very narrow well of a white spruce, while Brenda, Debbie and I took over the hollow under a large pine.

With the tents more or less secure and our gear stored inside, we tried to find wood to build a fire. Our jaws went slack as we realized the snow was already several inches deep, making it impossible to find dry wood or kindling. The llamas were lying down and rapidly disappearing under the snow. Every now and then, one of their big heads popped up like a snow-covered periscope and slowly dropped down when it became apparent there would be no grazing or walking that evening.

We could have used a fire, but I didn't recall seeing an axe in the provisions the llamas were carrying. I was wondering how we'd stay warm; we'd lost the battle on 'dry' a long time earlier. Our one small tarp hung limply over a large bush. Most of the space under it was taken up by the bush, leaving us trying to squeeze under the outer edges.

I can't remember what supper was, but it wasn't one of those mouth-watering meals made better by rigorous activity and dining al fresco. Our fire was limited to a small glow from a jam can, the only fire pit we could muster for the evening. We huddled together under the tarp telling jokes and trying to keep from getting too frightened. As branches of the bush poked our backsides, one of the women talked about hiking out, leaving the llamas with the guide. With darkness almost upon us, we realized that wasn't a safe option and the insurgency movement died a quick death. Brenda produced a small flask of brandy and divided it up. That ounce of brandy might have been the best I'd ever had. I think we were all looking for some liquid courage at that moment.

We went to bed to wait out the darkness; sleeping seemed like a long shot. There was barely room to roll out the sleeping bags and, with the tree roots at odd angles, the littlest movement would send someone rolling into their tent mates. After I'd counted the world's largest flock of sheep, dawn finally came to our beleaguered group. We crawled out of sleeping bags stiff, sore and cold; more than ready to hit the trail.

For breakfast we fired up the jam can and were soon dining on pancakes the size of silver dollars! By this time we were getting giddy and started to joke about my unexpected diet plan. We figured we'd all be a dress size smaller by the time we got out of this trip. To get in the spirit, we donned some new mountain clothes to stay warm – Glad garbage bags. With great creativity, we made Glad skirts to cover our legs and punched holes in others for our heads and arms to give our jackets extra warmth. The experts would say this was a bad idea; we would sweat inside the bag and end up even wetter; but we were having a Scarlet O'Hara moment by then. Frankly, we didn't give a damn.

When it was time to rouse the llamas and break camp, reloading them was a struggle. Apparently, unlike a pack horse or even a pet dog, a llama is a finely-tuned beast of burden. They will not get up if their load is more than a few ounces unbalanced. Our equipment was wet and, unlike us, weighed more than when we started.

Cheryl brought a fish scale out of her bag and painstakingly weighed each of the packs, pulling out things and adjusting the loads to make them balance. The process seemed to take forever and the human-llama bonds were dissolving before my eyes. More than one person was willing to say goodbye to their llama on the spot, but in the end we all agreed to finish as we started.

With our garbage bags flapping and our llamas shaking off their snow piles, we moved back down the mountain. The river crossings were even more bitterly cold with our wet gear, but we were spurred on by the thought of a warm coffee shop before day's end. Just before the parking lot came into sight, the sun popped out. We had survived, but I knew I would have trouble drumming up commitments for our next big adventure.

Within days, tales of our grand adventure had spread through our community and it had become a badge of honor to have survived the trip. The legend of the great llama trek lives to this day in certain circles in Calgary!

Stuck On Thompson Pass

"...You define a good flight by negatives. You didn't crash, you didn't get hijacked, you didn't throw up, you weren't late, and you weren't nauseated by the food." ~ Paul Theroux

Weather plays a role in many great travel stories. Canadians are by nature a northern people, and it's a badge of cultural honour to survive cold weather, high winds and deep snow. Canada isn't the only country to have severe winter weather. Shortly after my book, **The Business of Ecotourism,** was released, I was invited to be the keynote speaker at the Alaska Wilderness and Recreation Association conference in Valdez, Alaska. I was excited as I hadn't been to Alaska before and I had heard much about Valdez through the media coverage of the Exxon Valdez oil spill. It would be a winter trip, perhaps not an ideal time to see Alaska for the first time; but there's no off-season for a real traveller.

Most tourism industry conferences are held during slow times because that is when tourism business operators have fewer customers and time to focus on their business development. You need a great imagination to visit places in the off-season. To get an idea of a place in all its glory, I often have to picture the trees with leaves on them, imagine the birds that fill the sky and the flowers that cover the ground during summer months. Going in colder months often means few crowds and the chance for a real adventure. And that is what I got in Valdez.

I flew from Calgary to Anchorage and transferred to a small regional airline for the flight to Valdez. It was a bumpy flight with high winds, but seeing the mountain peaks standing as sentinels along the Prince William Sound was a treat. Valdez is the most northerly U.S. harbor that remains free of ice year-round. The contrast between the open water and the ten-foot high snow banks that rimmed the sidewalks was a surprise even to me who'd lived through some rough winters growing up in the prairies. The first evening, as I walked past the towering snow banks, I saw sea otters paddling in the moonlight around the boats tethered in the harbor. I was captivated by Valdez.

At most conferences, the host community will organize special events to showcase their hospitality and give you a peek at the best features of their region. On our second evening we were shuttled in school buses up the Richardson Highway over the Thompson Pass to a mountain lodge for a real Alaskan dinner. The drive over the winding mountain road, the fire in the cozy wooden chalet and the hearty meal gave us a glimpse into the rural Alaskan lifestyle. We laughed and enjoyed swapping stories of our past travel adventures. All too soon it was time to leave.

The wind was picking up as our little convoy of school buses and cars started down the mountain. Before long, the snow started, and the flakes became bigger and more numerous. The people on my bus weren't too worried; we were in a large vehicle and it wasn't a long drive back to town. The first sign that things were not going as planned was when we passed the snow plows idling on the side of the road. In hindsight we learned you should never, ever, pass the snow ploughs!

We inched slower and slower down the road until it became apparent we were in the middle of a full-on blizzard with white-out conditions on the top of a mountain pass; not something recommended in any travel guide. When the road disappeared from view, we came to a stop. There was a real possibility of driving off the road if we continued on.

We would be able to stay warm for awhile, but if we had to spend many hours in the bus, we could run out of fuel. A vehicle can quickly go from being a warm haven to a cold box when the engine is off. We needed to find a way off the mountain, and quickly. One brave man volunteered to get out and walk the road with us following him in the bus. The sharp blast of wind when the door opened made us realize this was a pretty significant gesture by our friend. Within minutes he was back, unable to see the road or stand up in the storm. Someone from the back of the bus suggested we wait for help to come to us. That idea died a quick death when we learned that the chief of police, the leader of the organization most equipped to mount that rescue effort, was our bus driver. Well, at least we weren't likely to get any speeding tickets that evening. I was hoping the community had a back-up rescue operation.

Morale on the bus was plummeting as we took stock of the situation and our wardrobes. We had dressed for a dinner out, not for an overnight back-country camping trip. We were going to need some serious group cuddling to stay warm.

Sometimes in situations like this, heroes come from unlikely places. From out of the swirling winds, a small car from behind us, inched forward until it was even with us. "I'm lower than you are, I think I can see the road," the driver called, an unlikely-looking heroine in her casual clothes and page-boy hairstyle. Off she went in her compact car, creeping forward at a snail's pace, but moving, nevertheless, and showing us the way. The relief we felt was palpable. It took a long, long time to get off the mountain and we cheered when the lights of Valdez came into view. We were safe.

The next day we heard that the woman who had lead our little convey off the mountain, had pulled muscles in her neck from the strain and effort she had put into leading us through those dreadful conditions. The conference continued and we were a closer group as a result of our evening adventures. I made a note to buy some high fashion fleece clothing for my next hinterland dinner outing!

Surviving A Coup

"I soon realized that no journey carries one far unless, as it extends into the world around us, it goes an equal distance into the world within."
~ *Lillian Smith*

Weather isn't the only thing that can put a traveller in danger. Sometimes political unrest or crime will put them in harm's way. Smart travellers will consult with their country's Foreign Affairs department when planning an international trip, to be aware of political problems. But what happens when you are already in the country and political disputes erupt?

This unlikely set of circumstances unfolded for Dr. Kelly Bricker in May 2000 when she was a professor at the University of the South Pacific in Suva, Fiji. As one of the world's experts on sustainable tourism and forestry, and a long-time adventure guide, Kelly was in the country to teach at the University, and to help establish an adventure tour company, Rivers Fiji, with her husband Nate.

Rivers Fiji was an initiative of OARS, one of the U.S.'s biggest and best rafting companies; SOTAR, a rafting and kayaking manufacturer, and Asia Pacific Management, a Fijian company manufacturing rafts in Fiji. Together with OARS founder George

Wendt, they had a vision for sustainable tourism development that he hoped to share with the Fijian communities in the area of the Wainikoroiluva (known as the 'Luva) and Upper Navua Rivers. Kelly and Nate had first visited Fiji in 1993 and were excited by the tropical rain forests, the beautiful rivers and starting an ecotourism business from the beginning. They came back several times, eventually teaming up with George Wendt, Glenn Lewman of SOTAR and Colin Philps of Asia Pacific Management to launch Rivers Fiji.

Kelly, Nate and George were adamant that Rivers Fiji would be developed in a way that protected the natural environment and enhanced the well-being of the people living in the area. They developed a guide training program to build a local labor force. They worked with local businesses to obtain food, and rented trucks and boats for shuttle services. Rivers Fiji set up a user fee to be paid to the native land owners so that they would see a direct economic benefit from the rafting activities which in turn would hopefully lead to protection of this wonderful landscape.

By many measures, Rivers Fiji has been successful. In 2000, it negotiated with the Fijian government to establish the Upper Navua Conservation Area, a unique public-private partnership that would protect the pristine river environment.

Kelly and Nate applied the same sustainability principles to internal business operations. Instead of soliciting job candidates through help-wanted ads, Kelly and Nate would ask the village leaders for their input. When there was a vacancy, Nate would ask the elders to suggest people that might be good employees. The village would put forward the names of those people they thought would make good guides, and the Rivers Fiji team would interview from this list to fill the position. Their approach garnered OARS and Rivers Fiji recognition from the World Tourism Organization in 2001.

Political tensions in Fiji erupted in May 19, 2000, when a rebel group led by George Speight took Prime Minister Mahendra Chaudhry and several Parliament members hostage. Speight had been involved in the local tourism association and was well-known to Kelly and other ecotourism professionals. The President Ratu Sir Kamisese Mara denounced the coup and declared a state of emergency.

The day things turned bad, Kelly was working at her university office. She learned that the situation off campus had gone from tense to dangerous. Word spread quickly that the government had been overthrown and that people should be careful. Kelly called Nate who told her to take a taxi home. With the streets in chaos, Kelly thought it would be safer to stay at the university for a few hours until things settled down.

When she left her office there were no taxis to be seen. Some of the tensions in the coup followed racial lines and the rebels had rounded up or scared off many of the taxi drivers who were Indo-Fijian in ancestry. Kelly started walking towards home, knowing she might face a very, very long walk.

"It was very eerie with only a couple of other stragglers on the streets," Kelly remembers. "Most people had decided to stay out of sight within the relative safety of their homes."

As Kelly made her way along the deserted streets, some of her students would dart out of their homes, and warn her to take cover, "What are you doing on the street?" they would whisper. "It's not safe."

Kelly was getting more concerned about how she would get home. Before she could panic, a fellow she knew from her tourism work drove by in a vehicle. Seeing Kelly, he ground to a stop and asked, "Why aren't you at home?" When she told him she was trying to get there, but had no ride, he replied, "Hop in, I'll drive you home. I am on good terms with the soldiers and the rebels. They will let me through the check-stops!" It turned out he did enjoy good relations with both sides and he was able to drive Kelly back to her home and the Rivers Fiji office.

When Kelly and her rescuer arrived at her home and the Rivers Fiji office, they found that Nate had a similar transportation dilemma on his hands. The Rivers Fiji staff had been in the office or on the river when the coup occurred couldn't get back to Suva where they lived. Kelly's Good Samaritan quickly volunteered to help out. He made his car available for a run back to Suva and took the Rivers Fiji Operations Manager and others back to their families. Without him, a lot of people would have been separated from their families at a very tense time.

The coup dragged on for several months. Tourism dried up as word reached the international press, and Kelly and Nate debated whether it was worth keeping Rivers Fiji open. George Wendt was prepared to support whatever decision they made. Since the violence associated with the coup was focussed in Suva and hadn't spread throughout the country, Kelly and Nate wanted to keep the company running so that the local villagers would not be left without any income or business activity. As the coup unfolded, Nate used the time to give the staff extra training. Hotels, their rooms empty, were happy to send their staff out to Rivers Fiji for additional training.

Kelly met with other tourism professionals to discuss how they would attract people back to the country when the coup was finally over. "We had a media and a marketing plan all ready for the time when we felt we could attract international travellers again," she said. "We worked diligently to communicate what was actually happening in the country to various State Departments."

Not all tourism organizations were favorably viewed by the coup leaders. The senior manager of one lodge was kidnapped by the rebels and held for many days while they debated who owned his property. The challenge was less for Rivers Fiji staff as they moved around the country. The rebels liked the company's philosophy so when they saw the Rivers Fiji vehicle logo or recognized the staff, they would let them pass through the roadblocks. The company kept operating.

"It was a very strange time," Kelly recalled, "If it had been anywhere else, there would have been a lot of people dead. But we learned the Fijians are very polite people; even with the strong political disagreements, very few people were injured. I don't think I could live under that uncertainty for a long time. Several times we were asked to leave the university for fear it was being taken over. It really wears you down; the stress, the not knowing what will come next."

Finally, in late July, the coup ended. George Speight was arrested and was eventually tried for treason. Normally a crime of this severity would merit a death sentence, but it was reduced to a lifetime banishment to a remote island. He is still there.

Near Death Experiences

"Every traveler has a home of his own, and he learns to appreciate it the more from his wandering." ~ *Charles Dickens*

We all know there is greater risk of being injured in the drive to the airport than in flying, yet many of us are nervous flyers, especially when it comes to small planes. One of my close friends, Carol Petersen, learned that when someone says, "one person in a million will be in an airplane crash," you could be that one person.

Carol has one of those jobs that people envy. As founder of Nature Encounters Tours and Travels, she takes groups of people on trips to some of the world's hottest wildlife-watching destinations. She has been to Africa dozens of times and while it's her favorite place to visit, she came close to ending her life there.

She arrived in Zimbabwe in September 1999 with a group eager to get into the bush for some wildlife viewing. Experienced African travellers know things don't always go according to plan on this beautiful continent and this trip was to be no exception. President Robert Mugabe simply "borrowed" the plane that was used for scheduled flights between Harare and Lake Kariba, Carol's flight.

With her flight plans in disarray, Carol found a charter aircraft that could fly her group to Lake Kariba. Unfortunately, it held twelve passengers and with Carol, her group numbered 13. Carol put her group on the plane and found another seat for herself on a small charter aircraft leaving later that day.

Carol really missed the camaraderie of her group when she found herself joining a couple of German hunters, a chain-smoking English woman, and a devastatingly good-looking French pilot. Carol was given the co-pilot seat, and she settled in for the quick jaunt to Kariba.

Shortly after take off, Carol's world shifted on her axis. The landing gear broke as it retracted. It wasn't apparent to Carol and the other passengers at first how serious the situation was. The pilot circled the Harare Charles Prince airport, and made several dive bombs at the runway, hoping to use the rapid speed to snap the landing gear into position for a landing.

His maneuvers didn't appear to work, and the pilot, in a moment of great understatement, announced in a very controlled and relaxed voice, "We have zee small problem with the landing gears, and we zwill need to do a very special landing."

There was a second of stunned silence, and then a small voice from the rear of the plane asked, "Is that a crash landing?"

"Oui," the pilot responded.

Carol and the other passengers were now officially worried. The pilot lined up an approach for a practice fly-by of the runway.

"Have you done this before?" Carol asked.

"I took this in training school," he replied.

"He didn't exactly answer my question, but I decided not to ask anything more in case I didn't like the answer," Carol said.

After four practice runs, the pilot was ready to try landing the plane on its belly; a risky procedure. He announced, "Oh good. Zee fire department is here." Carol looked out the window to see a single fireman with an oversized helmet and a small fire extinguisher.

"All that was missing was the Dalmatian dog standing next to him," Carol recalled with a laugh. "It wasn't the number of firemen I would have expected to respond to an emergency landing."

The pilot told them to assume the crash position as they started their descent.

"I was raised a Lutheran and I was praying now," Carol said, "I made all sorts of promises to be a better person if God would protect me in this landing. I was so afraid."

When the plane reached the runway, the pilot's practice had paid off. The belly of the plane rubbed along the tarmac and skidded off the end of the runway into the adrenaline grass.

"I was afraid the plane would flip once it made contact with the tarmac and there would be a horrible crash," Carol said. "For some reason, all I could think about was what would happen if I broke my arm. As a photographer, I wouldn't be able to take pictures. Then I remembered that it might not matter since I could be dead. It's crazy the things you think about in a time like that."

When the plane finally came to a stop, there was much rejoicing on board until the pilot's voice ripped through the melee, "Get out! Fire might break out!"

Everyone piled out the plane's small door. Carol said, "I scratched my arm getting out, and I still have the scar from it."

The other passengers escaped without any physical marks, but they were not unaffected. The chain-smoker was puffing frantically. One of the Germans was lying on the tarmac while someone rubbed her feet.

"These people who had annoyed me so much when I had boarded the flight now felt like my best friends," Carol said, "We were all so happy just to be alive." The fireman raced up with the fire extinguisher, but there was nothing for him to do. The ambulance arrived shortly after, but a quick check showed that cups of hot tea were sufficient medical care.

Carol had to go back into the terminal and make plans to get on another flight to rejoin her group in Lake Kariba. She checked out the landing gear on this plane carefully!

While Carol was boarding her second flight of the day, her group, which included her mother, had been told only the obvious – Carol's plane had crashed. There had been no other information available on the passengers, so when Carol showed up alive and well, she was met with many tears, mostly from Carol's mother who had lost her husband, Carol's father, nine months earlier.

Carol still leads trips to Africa several times a year. Her misadventure that day in Harare changed something in her. "I have complete faith that someone is looking after me. I realize that everything is supposed to happen for a reason. I guess I'm more of a fatalist now. I judged those people on the plane before I even knew them; I don't like hunters and smokers, but they are just people like me. I realized that I was lucky to have more time on the planet." So Carol continues to travel in small planes, but she says, "I'm always relieved to see fixed landing gear and I always pay special attention at takeoff!"

Making It Real

"Travel is the most private of pleasures. There is no greater bore than the travel bore. We do not in the least want to hear what he has seen in Hong-Kong." ~ Vita Sackville-West

Most people's travel experiences will not be life and death, but they will often be changed by them in small ways. Getting a chance to meet new people or try on other lifestyles is a novelty that attracts many travellers. In our world it is increasingly difficult to find such encounters, but they are still there if you look. Sometimes authentic travel experiences come in unexpected ways, and in locations that aren't seen on glitzy travel brochures. Carol Kline of North Carolina has been educating people for years on the philosophy of travel, but recently had the chance to convey more than travel theory to her students.

"Many people don't understand the role University Extension departments play in rural communities," Carol says, "They think we organize 4H, but there is so much more." Carol, a professor at North Carolina State University, has been involved in Extension activities for several years. Part of her job is to help more than 50 small communities with their economic development, something she enjoys; but the scope of her mandate can be overwhelming. "Do the math! With more than 50 communities to help and only 52 weeks in a year, you can't spend much time with any one community," she says.

Carol was also feeling burnt out with her overwhelming work duties. Her class on tourism planning was popular, but she was tired of teaching the same material over and over. In a moment of inspiration she realized she could use one problem to solve another. She would turn her class into a learning laboratory and ask the students to create an actual tourism strategic plan for the communities found in North Carolina's Pamlico County. This region had relatively little tourism development and community leaders wanted to create a plan before outsiders shaped the direction of the county with their purchasing decisions.

Pamlico County is 340 square miles of land and 225 square miles of water. People make their living from logging, fishing and farming; and little has changed in the past 50 years. The largest town is Oriental with 900 residents. Its wonderful harbor and favorable winds have earned it the label of sailing capital of North Carolina. Kayaking is another popular pastime, with several hundred miles of paddling routes in the area.

Carol was able to get approval for her plans to take the students into the community to do an actual strategic plan; she was also successful in squeezing out a small grant to cover the additional costs. She titled her course, "Tourism Planning: Keeping It Real" and prepared to hit the road.

Lectures were scheduled for three hours once a week and three trips to Pamlico County were planned. Half the students would do the first field trip, the other half would go on the second trip, and everyone would take the final trip when the complete plan would be presented. "It took a little extra effort to figure out how to divide the planning process into the thirteen week academic calendar, but it came together," Carol said.

Students interviewed tourism business owners, government officials and residents. "We discovered that about half of the locals did not want more tourists," Carol remembers. Instead of reading about abstract tourism concepts the students were now faced with solving some prickly problems on their own. It was a sobering realization for them to find that not everyone was as excited as they were about the tourism plan. "So what are you going to do now?" Carol challenged her students.

The students were up to it, going into overdrive searching for creative solutions to allow the businesses who wanted more tourists to expand without taking away from the traditional Pamlico life.

"It was a lot of hard work, but it was the best class I've taught," Carol said. One tourism company, Downeast Destinations, gained momentum as a result of the process and the Oriental Tourism Board created its own action plan with many of the strategies in the county plan. Carol said, "It was great to see the community embrace the students' work and know that an innovative approach had helped both rural North Carolina and the students."

Section Two - Wildlife

"I have never been in a natural place and felt that was a waste of time. I never have. If I'm walking around a desert or whatever, every second is worthwhile."
~ *Viggo Mortensen*

Don't Feed The Bears, *page 40*

Most of us hope to encounter wild animals on our holidays and at the same time are terrified we might. We can watch excellent documentaries and travelogues on TV or cruise YouTube for incredible footage of animal behaviors; but watching and participating are two entirely different things. You can watch an elephant charge a hundred times on TV and, while it may make you reach for another cold one, the excitement level is mild compared to what you feel seeing an elephant in the wild.

Travel is excellent at taking you out of your comfort zone and discovering a different side of your personality. On my first African safari, I was terrified at how close some of the animals came. This was no zoo and there were no guarantees bad things wouldn't happen. At the same time, though, I felt alive in ways I had never felt before.

I had reached the relatively ripe old age of 28 and yet I missed the exhilaration that comes from feeling a part of the animal kingdom and not knowing if you will come out on top. A cold Coke never tastes as sweet as when you've hiked through 40 degree Celsius temperatures for hours, looking for the elusive desert rhino. A towel never feels as soft as when you finish an impromptu swim in an African river, knowing that you were only kept safe by your guides circling in a motor boat.

Risk managers and insurance companies have taken some of the fun and much of the danger out of adventure travel, but there are still opportunities to see wildlife up-close. You will appreciate animals more after an intimate encounter especially if you have the benefit of a great guide to tell you more about what you are seeing and hearing. Some people find these experiences so profound it changes their lives forever. I know of more than one person who has gone on an African safari or a wilderness trip and come home to shake up their lives, jobs and even their relationships. In this section, we look at some great tales of wildlife encounters and the impact they had on me and other travellers.

Youthful Adventures

"And that's the wonderful thing about family travel: it provides you with experiences that will remain locked forever in the scar·tissue of your mind." ~ Dave Barry

I started travelling early and from my earliest recollections, I loved animals and seeing wildlife was always the high point of any trip. My parents would bundle my brother, sister and I into the car every summer for a meticulously-planned, week-long vacation, usually to the mountains. This was before credit cards were common. My parents had one for gas, but frequent flat tires meant there wasn't any extra money for frills. My parents took up camping in the 70s, not out of any love of the outdoors, but as a way to stretch their vacation dollars.

It wasn't a hardship at the time, but I wince when I recall how we crammed all five of us and an active dog into a nine by nine foot canvas tent. It had a center pole that held up the tent and served as a dividing line for the sleeping bags. My parents lay on one side, my brother and I on the other and my sister, being the smallest, got the unfortunate spot at the foot of the 'bed'. We used cheap air mattresses that would invariably leak, usually on alternate nights so that there was never any one night where everyone was comfortable.

Our sleeping bags were never warm enough and were often damp from the leaky, car top carrier. My dad put sheets of plastic over the bags to keep us warm. It worked although we were usually damp by morning from the condensation under the plastic. Even then, I could see the appeal of short term gain for long term pain!

Our family never had a cook stove or a proper axe. Dinner was Sloppy Joes and hotdogs cooked over the fire. It was primitive and I loved it. I went to the interpretative programs at every campground and dreamed about one day wearing a park ranger's uniform.

I wanted more than one week of real camping in a year, so my parents would sometimes let me pitch the tent in the backyard and have friends sleep over.

One night I had my girlfriend Donna over for a sleep out. We had Pepper, my high energy Beagle, with us for protection. In a move that proved to not be well thought out, I tied Pepper to the only solid thing in the tent, the center pole. It seemed like a good idea at the time.

All went well until Pepper heard a noise outside the tent. He probably interpreted it as food for his never-ending appetite. He burrowed that hound nose into the small hole where the zippers meet, and within seconds he burst free, dragging our tent pole behind him.

The tent was sinking fast. Knowing how hard Pepper was to catch, I was on my feet and out the tent door in hot pursuit, just as the tent came down on Donna. The sound of the tent pole clanging behind him on his leash made Pepper run faster. My parents, who were watching the late night news, looked out the front-room window to see their dog running down the street with a tent pole dragging behind him, followed by me in my pajamas in hot pursuit. I don't think they stopped laughing for a week.

I learned two important lessons that night. Never tie your dog to the tent pole and never give up camping because things don't turn out as you expect.

When I turned 17 I was allowed to go camping with my two best friends, Lotus and another Carol. We packed up that same sturdy tent and headed west to the mountains. First stop was my future home city, Calgary, where heavy rains threatened to ruin our sleeping bags and our plans. We made new mattress covers with Glad garbage bags. That was the start of a long love affair with this versatile and trusty camper's friend.

After a day in the big city we headed to Banff and Yoho National Parks for some "real" camping. I was the only one who had been to the mountains before, and I was busy giving out advice along with the tent pegs on what to do if we spotted a bear. "In no situations should you run away from the bear. Stay calm and make lots of noise," were my wise words to Lotus who was more than a little nervous about this wilderness foray.

As night fell, we built a large, crackling fire. Attracted by our fire building skills, a couple of guys from Chicago wandered over to chat around the picnic table. They hadn't been in the mountains before so we took great delight in our roles as mountain women, telling them how to behave if they were lucky enough to encounter any wildlife. Our bravado was shot to hell in a few short minutes when Lotus looked across the campfire and asked, "Isn't that a bear over there?" Unfortunately her eyesight was 20/20 and the bear was headed our way.

Disregarding our own advice, Carol and I screamed and jumped on the picnic table like some cartoon reaction to a mouse in the room. In hindsight, it was a pretty foolish response to a bear. The guys from Chicago remained calm and waved their arms around to shoo the bear away. The bear realized this was a group he wanted nothing to do with and disappeared into the night.

There was no chance of anyone sleeping in the tent that night so Carol, Lotus and I dozed off and on in the small, cramped quarters of my tiny frog-green Gremlin, never comfortable to begin with. It was a bonding experience for me and my friends, but Lotus never went camping again.

Don't Feed The Bears

"Some national parks have long waiting lists for camping reservations. When you have to wait a year to sleep next to a tree, something is wrong."
~ George Carlin

I am not the only person to have a great bear story. Catching a glimpse of the large, furry carnivores is the highlight of many people's visit to the forests of Canada and the United States.

Bears have a healthy respect for humans and will usually go out of their way to avoid people. Unfortunately, every now and then someone gets the worst in a bear encounter, and their story ends up as a dramatic newspaper headline. Most people will never actually see a bear, but they are in constant fear that they will be attacked while hiking or picnicking.

Miles Phillips, an expert in nature tourism development for Texas A & M University's Extension Department, discovered how powerful a bear encounter could be when he was leading a group of canoeists on a week-long paddle of the Boundary Waters area of Northeastern Minnesota.

National Geographic named the Boundary Waters area as one of the fifty destinations of a lifetime. It has more than 1,000 lakes and streams, and more than 2,500 kilometres (1,500 miles) of canoe trails. There are waterfalls, rocky outcrops, verdant forests and little sign of human presence. No power lines, roads or motorized craft are allowed in the one million acre wilderness area. It is one of the largest nesting areas in the lower 48 states for bald eagles and visitors will usually have the chance to see bear, moose, beaver and many other animals and birds up-close.

Miles is comfortable in the wilderness of northern Minnesota and a bit of a joker. He spent a lot of time hiking and hunting in the woods when he was growing up. Some of his fellow paddlers on this trip were less used to the outdoors, and in a mischievous spirit he filled them with bear stories including his personal experiences of bears coming into camp.

One evening after dinner, near the end of the trip, Miles was fishing on the lake. "I could hear someone calling my name very faintly from camp. I paddled closer to camp and heard someone yelling that a bear was in our gear." Miles said. Skeptical because of all the bear stories he had told, he paddled to shore and sneaked up quietly to see what was happening. There really was a bear and it was ransacking the camp!

"We had not yet hung our pack high; it was still about five feet off the ground on a branch. We watched the bear stand up and, with one paw, rip open the heavy canvas Duluth Sack with our food in it," Miles said. "I started yelling and startled him. He ran into the brush with the pack, but the bag split open and our food fell out."

Miles walked up to get the food, but the bear was not giving up. It moved up behind a tree near the food and Miles backed off.

"He would reach around the tree with one paw, snag some food and pull it around to the back of the tree. This went on a few times until it became obvious we were not going to get our food back," Miles lamented.

"We threw our remaining gear in the canoes and paddled across the lake to a campfire we had spotted earlier. It was a group of dads and their kids. We explained what had happened and they let us set up camp next to them. They shared some snacks with us and we dozed off," Miles said.

The next day Miles and his friends had to make the difficult decision of what to do next. They were hungry, had little chance of getting more food, and it was at least a day of hard paddling to get back to civilization.

"We decided the best thing was to paddle as hard as we could all day and get back as soon as we could. It was hard; we were hungry and sore from all the effort," Miles remembered. "And in a real twist of irony, the last lake we came to was called Lake Disappointment!"

It was a fitting end to a trip cut short. Much later, one of Miles' friends said he had the best time on that trip because of all the great travel stories he had to tell. A bear encounter can snap things into focus for us very quickly. Isn't the chance to reflect on our experiences once we get back in our everyday world one of the best things about travel?

The 'Easy' Bezi

"It is the little bits of things that fret and worry us; we can dodge an elephant, but we can't a fly." ~ *Josh Bill*

Encounters with large animals always make an impression on travellers. The risk, real or perceived, make for tales frequently retold by travellers to their friends and family back home. Miles' misadventures with a bear were great fodder for his friend's travel tales and made it a better vacation, at least in the re-telling.

Watching animals has been the focus of many of my trips, so I have probably found myself in more unusual situations than many people. As I discovered on one of my wildlife safaris, having to face real danger strips away many of our civilized responses. It lets us meet our inner survivalist. Dialing 911 is not an option in the bush. I think the confidence and relief one feels after a lucky escape gives a person a new-found appreciation for life and shakes off the tedium that often accompanies our workaday world.

I remember that feeling after courting disaster in one particularly-close elephant encounter and how shocked I'd been that something like that had happened to me, someone who always plans for every outcome. I'd been to Africa several times, but never to Zimbabwe, home of the famous Zambezi River. Several of my friends had canoed the 'Bezi' and assured me it was a wildlife experience like no other; something I shouldn't miss. I've never been a great paddler and my nerve for water adventures runs into the 'cluck, cluck' category, but everyone said it would be a piece of cake. I've always found that when someone uses that expression they are usually bad bakers and you should proceed with caution.

Safaris in Zimbabwe are much different than those in eastern Africa where you bump around the savannah in Land Rovers and the ubiquitous white mini-van. In Zimbabwe you're able to leave the vehicles and walk among the animals. The guides carry reassuringly-large rifles and you can count on having several members of the big five – elephant, rhino, buffalo, hippo and lion – strolling through your safari camp at any time of the day or night. Sleep is often interrupted by the sound of large branches splitting or eerie night calls. You play 'what's that sound?' with your tent-mate.

The unsettling feeling of leaving the security of camp and being at one with God's creatures can't be conveyed by a travel brochure. You soon understand why our ancestors took some time to come out of the trees. We're smaller than lots of predators and don't run all that fast, something I learned first-hand.

One day a stomach bug hit our safari group and my husband, Colin, and another camper, Lois, were hit particularly hard. When I awoke that morning to the sounds of retching all around me, I knew we wouldn't make a full day of paddling. After all, how do you paddle and puke at the same time?

The guides shuttled the sickest guests along with their spouses off to the next camp to rest. I was happy to spend a day in camp and Colin was too green to much care what we did with him. Once settled in camp, James, the guide assigned to watch over sick bay, suggested that Lois' husband, Phil and I follow him across a fallen tree to a nearby island to bird watch. We could enjoy some wildlife watching and James could keep an eye on camp and our sick compatriots. It sounded like a great plan, so we grabbed our binoculars and cameras and headed out.

We'd spotted only a few birds before we looked back at camp to see two bull elephants lumbering among the canvas tents. Lois and Colin had prudently taken shelter behind a large tree. They were more than a little nervous about such large visitors and had no idea of how to move these big guys along. Saying 'shoo' seems a little inadequate in the face of several tons of pachyderm. James jumped up from his perch by the river and scurried back to camp to chase off the elephants, and keep his insurance premiums from escalating.

Phil and I had every faith in James's rescue skills and were enjoying our ringside seats for the mini-drama. We were sitting close to a ledge overlooking the river when the tall adrenaline grass behind us starting to rustle. Adrenaline grass is accurately named; it is tall and thick and your adrenaline often kicks in as something unexpected walks out of it. This was one of those times. After a few seconds of the stalks waving and crunching, the large grey head of an elephant appeared with apparently more behind it. Phil was elated at the thought of some close-up shots of a big bull. He knew that they were seldom aggressive as long as you don't corner them.

Unfortunately our good luck didn't hold. A few seconds later the grass rustled again and a much, much smaller elephant came into view. My heart leapt to my throat as it became clear we were looking at a cow-calf herd, not a couple of bachelors. We were in deep doo doo! Female elephants are extremely protective of their young, and this mamma was none too happy to see us.

As we started to back up, I was mentally evaluating our options and not liking any of them. Going forward would have meant we'd be flatter than road-kill in seconds. Backing up was going to put us into the Zambezi River very quickly. I recalled some enthusiastic tour guide telling me that the river had a crocodile density of one croc every square metre. The term 'crocodile infested' was not an understatement.

Fortunately, having rescued our spouses from their elephant encounter, James looked over to see us trying to avoid a nasty showdown. He ran for the tree bridge again, shaking his rifle in the air to get the elephants' attention.

The lead cow elephant was suitably impressed by the size of James' gun. She turned and led her group into the river. Better her than me, I thought, as she swam through the crocs to the other side.

I've always stressed the need for good guides in my tourism training workshops, but that day I was really glad I was travelling with the best. I was able to laugh about this experience later, but I learned in spades that paying extra for a good guide was as, or more important than hiring a good accountant for your taxes or a mechanic for your car.

Sharing The Trail

"The only reason I would take up jogging is so that I could hear heavy breathing again." ~ *Erma Bombeck*

After many years as a wilderness guide, Kirk Hoessle became president of Alaska Wildland Adventures, a small-group, natural history tour company with trips ranging from the protected areas of the Kenai Peninsula to Denali National Park in Alaska.

Kirk holds a degree in Environmental Education and is excellent interpreter of the environment, having worked for many years in interpretative design and planning. Kirk knows though that there are times when a good guide has to manage encounters with animals on the trail first and save the interpretation until for back at the lodge. He describes one his most memorable wildlife encounters:

A couple years ago, I lead one of our groups on a hike in the Chugach National Forest, near our Kenai Riverside Lodge in Alaska. We were hiking along the Russian River Trail. (By the way, we actually get this question a couple times a year: "Is this the same Russian River that they have in California?" We humans say the funniest things sometimes, don't we?) Well, it was approaching ten o'clock at night, but it was mid July, so the sun was still well above the horizon. It was, however, the time of day where the primary use of the trail transitions from humans to critters.

I was hiking near the front of a group of seven or eight, when we suddenly heard up ahead what sounded to me like the roar of a lion. Someone asked, "Is that a bear?" I said, "I don't know,

I've never heard anything quite like it. Let's hold up here and gather together."

We next heard big things moving swiftly through the willows, just ahead and off the trail to our left, a couple hundred feet away. I saw the blur of two brown things, running first one way and then another, and then we heard what sounded like the scream of a donkey (heehaw, heehaw!). Again I was asked, "What was that?", and as an experienced and trained Alaska wilderness guide, I was able to give a confident: "I don't know!"

Then, from ahead of us on the trail, where we needed to hike to get back to the lodge, came a pattering of footsteps. Rounding the curve and 60 or so feet ahead of us was a grizzly bear cub charging down the trail at us. So I said to everybody, "stay together, look big, yell loud, and slowly take a couple steps backward!" which is what you're supposed to do when you have a bear coming at you.

Well, in our enthusiasm, I think we overdid it a little. The little cub just freaked out by our presentation. It immediately stopped in its footsteps, stood up, and then ran off to the right of the trail and swiftly climbed to the top of a spruce tree, all the while screaming at the top of its voice like the crying of a human baby, another new sound of nature for me.

Then we heard bigger footsteps coming down the trail toward us, and, you guessed it, here comes the mamma bear. "Stay together, look real big and shout real loud!" I shouted as we took a couple more slow steps backward.

Well, we freaked her out, too. She stood up on the trail. Looked at us, looked up the tree at her little cub crying, looked back at us. Right about that time, a second cub stuck its head between the mama's legs as she was standing and gave us a good look over as well. It would have been the greatest picture, but of course none of us had photography on our mind.

She ran over to the base of the spruce tree, the second cub following. She called up to the cub, using some guttural language that was yet another new sound of nature for me. The little cub swiftly climbed down the tree and we heard the whining of the bears and the commotion in the bushes fade as the family retreated off to our right.

But the show was not over ... from ahead on the trail again came the sound of more footsteps, this time more determined that ever. Here came the mama moose, ears down, head forward and nostrils flared, obviously very upset. Well, for a charging bear you hold your ground and retreat slowly, but for a charging moose you get off the trail if you can and get out of the way. "Everybody up the hill, I shouted!" To the right of the trail was a steep incline and I herded everyone up between some tree stumps and just as the moose got to us I started swinging a thick tree branch I picked up as if it were a club. The group was all gathered behind me and I heard one woman say in a happy, chirpy voice, "Wow, Kirk, this is great. Does this happen all the time?" I said something like, "Lady, this isn't a movie, this is the real thing! We need to be very cautious right now!"

The moose stopped in front of my swinging stick, seemed to get control of itself, and stared us down. We put the scene together. We must have just walked into the scene of the grizzly chasing and killing a moose calf, and then the bear apparently got chased away by the angry mother moose. We were a surprise to them all, and none of them knew what to make of us.

After cornering us for some time, she then walked across the trail, back up through the bushes to the apparent kill site, and then she got all flustered again, because the next thing we knew, she was again charging down the trail right at us, head forward, ears bent, nostrils flared – blaming us for all her troubles in the world.

We again gave her the trail and retreated to our fortress between the stumps, and of course I again saved the group from being trampled by looking tough on the outside, freaking on the inside, and swinging my big stick. By this time, I think everybody caught on that we were potentially in big trouble.

Eventually – and I really don't know how much time had passed – she calmed down, walked back across the trail. When she put her head down and began nibbling the willows, some hundred feet or so away, we made our exit.

I lead the group up the slope and then parallel to the trail, heading toward our lodge. The problem was, we needed to cross paths with the route of the bear family, but by this time they were nowhere to be seen or heard. After about a hundred yards or so, I lead the group back down to the trail, and we sprinted for another quarter mile, just to get away from the war zone. We then made it back to the lodge with no further incident. I recall that we enjoyed a couple six packs of Alaskan Amber as we shared our fears and perceptions of the dramatic chain of events. A toast to a life of adventures aplenty!

Pooping Orangutans

"An adventure is only an inconvenience rightly considered." ~ G.K. Chesterton

As I learned on the Zambezi, a great guide will often make the difference between the trip of a lifetime, a so-so tour or a near-death experience. If you live in a city, you are used to dodging urban creatures, but your skill in spotting wildlife needs to be developed. You may be able to spot a bird or a small animal even if you can't identify it by name. You may not know what animal behavior you're watching. A guide can be your key to unlocking the secrets of Mother Nature. Good interpretation will have you hungering for more knowledge, marveling at the grand design of our wild places, and wondering how you fit into it.

I was visiting Sukau Rainforest Lodge in northern Borneo to celebrate the launch of **Saving Paradise: The Story of Sukau Rainforest Lodge**, a book I co-wrote with lodge owner Albert Teo. I love this lodge, nestled in the banks of the Kinabatangan River which is sometimes called the 'mini-Amazon'. With only 20 rooms and sitting areas tucked along the forest boardwalks, the lodge and its grounds feels at once cozy and exotic. I only had to stroll a few feet along the lodge boardwalks to find something in the forest worth watching.

Early each morning, the langurs will pass through the grounds. The hair on their heads comes to a mussed point, reminding me of the Grinch in Dr. Seuss' story. In the afternoon, you can spot the large Proboscis monkeys settling in along the river for the night. Their loud calls and their gigantic, noisy leaps among the trees reminded me of people staking out the best spots along a beach.

Night at the lodge is equally fascinating. You can hear the owls calling from their perch just outside the light of the lodge's lanterns, and the impromptu orchestra of insect noises.

If you tire of watching the wildlife near the lodge there are always plenty of other things to do. Every visitor gets the chance to tour the waterways by boat; or, if you want to go inland, there are some short hiking trails.

One morning, a group elected to do a hike near the water feature known as the Oxbow Lake. I chose to do another boat cruise. I love riding along in the small boats, feeling a bit like the Queen of the Nile, as I scan the river bank for wildlife and snap photos whenever the urge strikes. I will also admit to being a bit of a wuss. There are leeches in the forest, and I'm terrified of picking one up. I know they aren't fatal and removing them is relatively painless. A little salt sprinkled on a leech, and they drop right off, or so I'm told. I've seen the blood that runs down your limbs after they've left their calling card, and the thought of looking like the star of a horror film keeps me away from the forest during peak-leech times.

The breakfast buffet was in full swing by the time the walking group made its way back to the Lodge. Their guide, Mark, seemed a little bit irritated, and the group was talking rapidly. "We got pooped on by an orangutan," someone shouted. This was going to be a story worth hearing, and I moved closer to hear the details. "We had barely started hiking the trail when we found a mother orangutan and her baby," Mark explained, "They were high up a tree, but we were able to walk right under them."

I was guessing that the group wasn't thinking about Newton and his law of gravity when they crowded in for a closer look. "Suddenly the orangutan pooped and it all came falling down on us," Mark said, "I've even got poop in my ear!" We all laughed at that comment, although it didn't look like Mark shared in the hilarity.

I told him "Maybe getting pooped on is good luck."

Mark looked at me like I was crazy. I told him a story from when I had been a volunteer with the Calgary Zoo. The Zoo Director had been walking by the tiger enclosure one day when the tiger had turned close to the fence and sprayed a young man watching the animal. The man was furious at being covered in pee – tiger urine smells very strong – and I'm guessing you'd have your choice of any seat on the bus if you got on wearing "eau de tiger."

The fellow had looked around in anger and headed for the man with 'Zoo Director' on his name tag nearby. As he rushed over to complain, the Zoo Director knew a public relations opportunity when he saw it. "Did you know in some cultures, it's considered good luck to be sprayed by a tiger?" he asked. (He admitted later he couldn't name such a culture.)

"No, I didn't", the young man replied.

"Yes," the Zoo Director replied, "You are very lucky." Suddenly the young man's face was transformed and he went from being angry to pensive. Now he would have a story to tell his friends, and perhaps even a little luck would come his way.

I told Mark that maybe he could tell people that being pooped on by an orangutan was also good luck. "You Canadians are strange people," he said and went to wash his hair. I figured he was missing a marketing opportunity. Travel teaches us that

The Bat Cave

"My first rule of travel is never to go to a place that sounds like a medical condition and Critz is clearly an incurable disease involving flaking skin." ~ Bill Bryson

I had the chance to work on my perceptions of what is pleasant or constitutes a 'real' tourism attraction, when I was given the chance to visit the Gomantong Cave in northeast Borneo with large numbers of birds and bats. Caves like Gomantong are home to thousands of small birds known as swiftlets. Their nests are made from saliva mixed with feathers and other nest materials, and are highly prized as ingredients in birds-nest soup. A nest can be worth over $500US per kilogram so it is important to regulate collection so that over harvesting doesn't occur. The Gomantong Cave has been described by the World Wildlife Fund as one of the best managed edible birds-nest cave in the world.

The Gomantong Cave is also a popular tourist attraction. It's a unique chance to see how the bird's nest industry works, and to observe the delicate ecosystem of the cavern. I've always enjoyed seeing new bird species and I like bats, so it wasn't hard to convince me to add a visit to Gomantong Cave when I left Sukau Rainforest Lodge.

A stop at the visitor centre explained the intricacies of nest harvesting and the risks people take in climbing the fragile-looking rattan ladders and ropes to the cave's highest reaches. After a quick stop, we were off to see the Sumud Hitam, or the Black Nest Cave. It is a large cavern, 30 metres wide and 100 metres high, with raised boardwalks to make walking easier. I soon realized I underestimated the challenge in this adventure. The short walk to see the cave would turn out to be one of the longest walks of my life.

I entered the cave, gagging on the ammonia-fumes of bat guano permeating the stale air and feeling my feet sliding on the accumulated droppings of thousands of bats and birds. Wearing open-toe sport sandals may have been a good fashion choice in the morning, but made for precarious footing in the cave. In the corner of my eye, I caught the flash of red on the ground. Closer inspection with a flashlight showed the ground was alive with hundreds of cockroaches. I wished I hadn't looked.

Saat, our guide from Borneo EcoTours, pointed out there would be rats around who would eat the insects and snakes who would eat the rats. A very healthy ecosystem, but not exactly what I had anticipated when entering one of Borneo's newest ecotourism attractions.

"It's interesting, but slightly unpleasant," Saat said as he tightened his shirt around his neck, "If you look up, keep your mouth closed." Wise words I figured, knowing that the cave is home to hundreds of busy swiftlets who flew back and forth in their daily search for food.

When I entered the cave, I hadn't counted on almost falling on my rear end in bat droppings and enough cockroaches to keep me in therapy for years. Saat gallantly offered his hand to keep me upright; probably figuring, somewhat correctly, that the trip would be cut short if I fell down. We proceeded further into the cave to a sight that would have taken your breath away if you weren't already holding it.

The cave's walls sweep up over 100 metres (300 feet) with sunlight streaming in from openings at the top; it looked like a scene from Raiders of the Lost Ark. Swiftlets darted back and forth from their nests to the forest in their ongoing search for food. Bats moved about in darkened corners of the cave. Ladders and ropes lying idle, waiting for the next nesting season when skilled collectors would risk their lives to gather their bounty. In all, it was a stunning sight and one I am glad I didn't miss despite the perils of getting there.

I figured there was a life lesson in this experience. Like my trip to the Gomantong Cave, it may be necessary to endure a little unpleasantness, keep your mouth shut, risk falling on your rear and wade through some "droppings". However, if you hold true to your vision, you will be rewarded.

An Arctic Expedition

"I dislike feeling at home when I am abroad." ~ George Bernard Shaw

Why is it that sometimes the best trips require a little suffering? I can't say that all my senses were delighted by the visit to the Gomantong Caves, but I'm glad I made the effort to see this unique place. The same forces are in play for many types of adventure travel. While many people enjoy some vacation time with no more difficulties than deciding which tropical drink to sample next, the growth in adventure travel suggests to me that people are looking for something more. I think that people want to test their mettle and see what they can do when they are placed in unexpected circumstances or face physical hardships.

If you read the historical travelogues of explorers, the challenges these people faced as they sought out new destinations is mind-boggling. The technology available to modern travellers in clothing, communications and medicine means we can venture further with less preparation and fewer risks. A paper pusher by day can become an explorer, for a few weeks a year.

In 2004, I decided to push my boundaries and explore a part of the world historically unseen by mass tourists – Canada's Arctic. It might seem a strange choice since I get cold easily, but I have always been fascinated by the Arctic. When the opportunity arose to do an expedition cruise to Greenland and the Northwest Passage, I jumped at it.

I had seen some of the western Arctic early in my accounting career. As the fixed asset accountant, I had travelled to Tuktoyaktuk to count the drill-ships and shore-base buildings for an oil company. I was amazed to see a landscape almost as flat as the prairies I'd grown up in, but so different in so many other ways.

As the company Boeing 737 circled the short runway, I got my first view of the real north. The Arctic Ocean glittered in the distance, small ponds and lakes dotted the green muskeg. The sky was different, perhaps the light was flatter, but I felt like I was 'north' in a way that is difficult to explain. I didn't feel I would fall off the end of the earth, but it seemed like we were at the edge of a final frontier where man's presence wasn't a given.

Venturing into this wilderness requires a lot of planning and special skills if you hoped to return. Required arctic clothing included a parka rated to minus 50C. I was reminded of how unforgiving the arctic climate can be when I was required to carry this parka with me everywhere in the camp buildings, even if I wasn't going outside. The building was big enough that if a fire broke out while I was working in the office, I might not be able to get back to room to get my coat, and standing outside for a few minutes in winter weather could be dangerous. We couldn't all run off to the Holiday Inn while the fire department dealt with the problem!

My memories of those visits to the Arctic were good ones, so in 2004, I convinced Colin that spending our holiday north of the Arctic Circle would be so much better than working on our tans at 'normal' summer destinations. Peregrine Adventurers of Melbourne, Australia, runs a few small expedition cruises each summer and it seemed like the perfect way to see the north.

Hiring Russian ice-worthy research vessels, Peregrine takes its guests into places that are difficult to reach my land and air. They have the bonus of giving people a relatively comfortable place to stay each night. The *Akademik Ioffe* takes about 110 passengers and 53 crew, not exactly the Caribbean Princess.

We flew to Ottawa, met our trip leaders and boarded a flight the next morning to Iqualuit. At the Iqualuit airport, all the trip leaders immediately went into a quick team huddle with a lot of intense whispering. I knew the real adventure had begun! Sure enough, we were informed that our ship was stuck in ice and would not be meeting us as planned.

While the *Ioffe* waited for a Coast Guard icebreaker to escort it into port, we would need a place to stay and eat. A hundred-plus people on an unexpected layover in a large city is not a big deal. In a small northern community like Iqualuit; it IS a really big deal. There weren't enough hotel rooms for everyone.

Northern communities have a history of coping with the unexpected. Under the community's contingency plan, we could bunk at the community college residence since school wasn't in session. There was no one restaurant in town that could handle the catering, so several restaurants were given as large an order as they could handle with the hope that the total added up to enough supper for everyone.

While the rooms were readied and food cooked, we were given the chance to wander about town and do a little impromptu shopping. Seeing the juxtaposition between modern homes and more traditional structures was interesting, as was watching some of the craftspeople carve caribou antlers at the end of their driveway to sell to tourists. The fine workmanship of regional artisans was also on display at a local museum.

Peregrine Adventures promises its guests exceptional cooking, so an impromptu fast food buffet was a bit unexpected to start our expedition. But, given the circumstances, we were all happy to have warm food and a bed to sleep in. I've bunked in airports before, but there wasn't enough room for all of us to camp out at the Iqualuit airport lounge.

We passed the evening at the college getting regular updates on the ship's progress, and laughing over the suggested shower schedule. We had one towel to share among one hundred people. Word arrived that the icebreaker had reached our ship, and it was expected to reach the harbor by morning. Plans were made to shuttle our group on board in time for a hot breakfast. No doubt the local restaurant owners were relieved that they would not have to rustle up another meal.

After the delay, everyone was extremely excited about finally setting sail, so to speak. Of course we had no sails. Instead we had one of the world's most modern research vessels. The **Akademik Ioffe** is one of five Russian vessels built for scientific exploration of the north. It was built for sound research, and with its special horizontal and vertical stabilizers it could hold its position, even in rough seas, to within five metres. It also made for a very comfortable cruise as there wasn't the rolling and pitching you might expect from a smaller ship on rough seas.

Our ship's captain, a distinguished-looking Russian, was very proud of his craft and his crew. He was extremely safety orientated, a good thing when you are a long, long way from help. Bobbing about in life boats in Arctic conditions is no guarantee of survival.

Our captain had been trained in avoiding polar ice. The vessel was reinforced to withstand some ice contact, but it wasn't an icebreaker. The insurance providers for the tour company forbid the vessel to sail in anything greater than forty percent ice coverage when tourists were on board. Imagine the captain's consternation when our trip leader, Stan, coaxed him time and time again to get closer to the ice. The ice was where the animals were often found, and we had come to see the arctic wildlife. Stan used to joke that he stood outside the captain's room at night, chanting "ice is nice" as he slept.

Life on the **Akademik Ioffe** quickly fell into a regular routine. The intercoms would crackle to life with Stan's "Good morning! It is a lovely five degrees Celsius outside, and a polar bear has been spotted off the starboard side." We'd scramble from our bunks, grabbing our binoculars and our clothes as we tumbled out the door to see what delights were on display that day. Sleeping in would have been difficult, but we didn't mind; the scenery was magnificent and we didn't want to miss a minute of it.

This is an unfamiliar part of the world. At first I was surprised to see large mountains and glaciers. As we got used to seeing these spectacular vistas and stopped snapping pictures every few minutes, we turned our focus to another important feature of the ships, the meals.

The chefs were world class. We soon learned, that in terms of ship rules, safety is Number One, but almost as important was the rule not to be late for a meal. Even the guides lived in fear of lingering too long on an outing and causing a delay in the meals. I soon learned that if the cooks aren't happy, ain't nobody happy on an expedition!

The *Ioffe* came with a fleet of Zodiac inflatable boats, and every day we would pile on our warm outerwear and line up for our chance to bob around in the ocean. At sea, we would head to the edge of the ice and look for polar bears. We weren't disappointed; we saw more than 50 bears in just over a week. Seeing them in their natural environments is one of the world's best wildlife experiences.

I believe I set a ship record for the number of layers I was able to put on before these outings. Arctic summers are cool, especially when you are a few inches from the chilly Arctic ocean, and we would often sit without moving for a couple of hours at a time. I would entertain Colin with my reverse striptease as I carefully added more layers to get maximum warmth. On the coldest days, I had nine layers of clothing on my upper body and seven layers on the bottom. I had to plan my bathroom breaks with great care, but I was warm enough to turn my full attention to wildlife watching. What a spectacle it was!

You don't realize how athletic a polar bear is until you see it swim. They cover long distances searching for seals, their main food source. Bears are no match for the speed of seals in the water so they need to hunt on the ice where they can sneak up on their prey. This is why climate change is so disastrous for the bears. The ice forms later and is farther away.

Our guides told us bears have drowned trying to swim out to the ice, distances that were too great for them. Seeing the bears swimming and lazing about on the ice was even more special when I realized how endangered they are.

As much as we enjoyed watching the bears, we realized that is we got too close, we would be endangered. Our boats always travelled in pairs and one of the guides would carry a rifle. I didn't think there was a need to use the guns, the guides kept us a safe distance from the bears; but the insurance providers forbid us to travel without the guns.

Our shore excursions were an interesting mixture of exploration and safety precautions. With the *Ioffe's* small size, we could stop the ship where we wanted and offload the Zodiacs to explore. Some of our hikes in Greenland were in places that the company guides had never hiked. It was exciting to realize we were striking out on our own, not using an established hiking trail.

Before we could go ashore, our guides and gun bearers would land and patrol for polar bears. Once they were sure there were no bears in the area, we got the all clear and our Zodiacs would go to shore and offload. Usually this was an uneventful occurrence, but the day we stopped at Devon Island, we were reminded of how unpredictable the north can be.

Stan, our lead guide, had been scanning the horizon as he walked the shore looking for bears. He spotted a polar bear and was about to return to the boat, when another of our boats came from the opposite direction, startling the bear. The bear started to run away from the new boat, straight for Stan.

Stan was on a peninsula, and he decided the wisest course was not to run back to his boat and risk being overtaken by the bear. He cut across the peninsula to the ocean where we could circle around in our boat and pick him up. When we picked him up, the adrenaline was still coursing through his system. The last thing anyone wanted was to harm the bear or to be harmed by the bear. We were happy that the morning ended with nothing more than a good story to tell.

For obvious reasons, that hike was cancelled, so we turned the boats towards a nearby island with several dozen walruses. I've always loved walruses; their long tusks and whiskers give them a friendly-looking face. In reality, though, they aren't that good natured. They can be very aggressive if disturbed, and those tusks are formidable weapons.

This morning we were content to bob a short distance off shore and listen to their grunts and groans as they jostled for the best sunbathing spots at the top of the small rock outcrop. Being downwind of the walruses provides an extra dimension to wildlife watching. Eating a steady diet of raw seafood and lying in close quarters with your neighbors is a sure-fire recipe for odiferous smells. It was far from pleasant to get a strong whiff of the walruses, but at the same time it reminded me that we were in a great Canadian wilderness.

It was an incredible privilege to experience this part of Canada's heritage, and realizing that few others would get a similar chance made me sad. Yes, at times it had been uncomfortable. I'd had to use a scarf to keep from swallowing more than my daily recommended allowance of flying insects, and I found I could not relax when the ship creaked and groaned in heavy ice, but this was one of the best trips of my life. I loved the spontaneity that came from exploring areas that saw few if any tourists, and I was proud that it was part of the country I call home. I was eager to learn more about the other frontiers waiting to be explored right here in Canada, and I realized I didn't need to travel across continents to find the exotic. It was living right next door.

Bambi's Mother Fights Back

"I ask people why they have deer heads on their walls. They always say because it's such a beautiful animal. There you go. I think my mother is attractive, but I have photographs of her." ~ *Ellen DeGeneres*

You don't have to travel to the Arctic or Africa to have great wildlife encounters. Often, the common wildlife species near our own communities can provide a great travel experience. Observing small animals, like squirrels, or birds can add much pleasure to a holiday. Deer are relatively easy to spot. While we think of these animals as mild-mannered ungulates, they can sometimes surprise us with behaviors we may associate with much fiercer animals, and give us a travel experience we won't soon forget.

I love to horseback ride when I travel, and nothing relaxes me as much as a couple of hours in the saddle. I think horses have an amazing sense of intuition. They seem to be able to read the rider's intent on almost a mystical level, and act on your intent before you can even articulate a command. Horses are also very aware of their environment, and have a very healthy interest in self-preservation, something that was brought home to me one day in July 2003.

There was a trail riding outfitter a few kilometres from my cabin in the Rocky Mountains. I started hiding out there for brief respites from the never-ending renovations that come when you buy a cabin quaintly labeled 'a handyman special'. Shortly after taking on the cabin, I became a frequent rider at the stables and then started helping out, first, saddling horses, then loading customers, and eventually riding along as an extra hand. Most of these rides were uneventful, and the days passed in a blur of gentle rides and pleasant conversations with tourists from around the world.

While Canadian winters are notorious for their bone-chilling cold (or at least they were until global warming got going), there is nothing nicer than a Canadian summer. The early mornings are fresh, the grass seems greener, and the way the sun hits the mountain as it rises, can turn anyone into a poet.

The first ride of the morning was always my favorite because the air is moist and cool, and there is a better chance of seeing wildlife. Rick, the owner and head guide, liked wildlife as much as the next person, but preferred his wildlife viewing at a distance. While many riders would ask about the possibility of seeing bears, usually in a tremulous voice, Rick would tell people the biggest threat to the horses came from the lowly grouse.

These game birds seemed to have a really strange sense of retribution; they would wait until the horses were almost upon them, before they would fly up and away. The sudden burst of flying bird would spook all but the steadiest of horses, and often there would be a few minutes of horse mayhem before everyone could gather their reins and their nerves, and get back in line. To avoid these problems, Rick had taken to bringing his dog, Hunter, along on the early rides. Hunter, a well-trained Lab, would dart back and forth into the bushes, sniffing her way back to the trail periodically, to make sure we were still around.

On this particular day, I was riding Spot, a sturdy Paint horse with, as you might guess, a rather large spot on his side. We were pulling up the rear behind a couple of young women from the United Kingdom. They had ridden a bit, but this was their first horseback trip in the mountains. The steady sound of their voices as they asked questions about the region was interrupted as all hell suddenly broke loose.

Out of the corner of my eye, I could see a large, brown, furry creature headed our way at great speed. I was wondering what was going on but was relieved to see it wasn't a bear coming at us; bears didn't come in that shade of brown. But I wasn't able to identify what it was.

Spot wasn't waiting around for the taxonomical identification. He broke into a run, right into the bum of the horse in front of him! Hey, this fight or flight thing is not an exact science, and most dude ranch horses spend their days in a kind of trail-induced trance, following the horse in front of them kilometre after kilometre.

Spot had managed to start a chain reaction of horses spooking, until they were all headed past Rick, and his horse, River. River was a legend at the stables; he had gotten Rick out of several tight situations, even facing down a grizzly bear at one point. Instead of running forward, Rick and River stopped the rush, and swung around to see what creature was after us. Imagine our bemusement when we found ourselves facing a very angry deer! It looked like a normal deer in size and color, but the body language was much different. It was snorting and pawing the ground, almost daring us to get any nearer.

Hunter, the dog, had apparently gotten too close to this deer, and she had young nearby. She was brave, and more than ready to take on our group even though we were much bigger than her. She charged our group again, which by now had slowed to a walk. The horses were a little confused as to why this normally mild-mannered deer was running at them and snorting. As the rider on the last horse in the chain, I had the unsettling experience of wondering if I was going to be one of those odd news tidbits that close a news broadcast. You know, a "woman mauled by deer" clip that that might fill in the last few seconds before broadcasters cut to the next show.

In a few minutes, we were far enough away that the deer relaxed and went back to her young. Never again will I think of deer as shy creatures. I realized that not giving all animals their space, no matter how small or meek they might first appear to be, can have unexpected reactions.

Section Three – People and Places

"If man was logical, he would ride side saddle."
~ *Author Unknown*

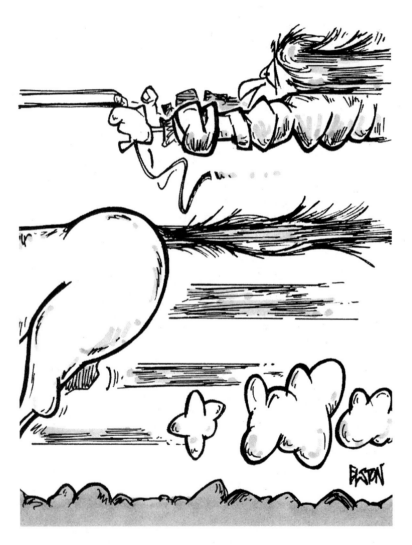

Trying On Other People's Lives, *page 107*

Getting a chance to meet new people is a big part of the travel experience. We're naturally curious about people who live in other parts of the world, and we want to learn more about their lives.

David Brooks, author of **Bobos in Paradise**, says that travellers today often want to try on other people's lives. These new travellers are curious about these foreigners. They want to know how people make a living, what they do for fun, and how they interact with their landscape. Meeting local people and being exposed to their customs and traditions can add colorful experiences to any trip.

Sometimes the experiences that make the biggest impressions come from our interactions not with local people, but with our travelling companions. We all like to think we are cool under pressure, don't make snap judgments about other people or cultures, and know how to share. You probably recognize this as the sort of stuff that you had to learn in kindergarten to get along with the other kids.

My experience has been that people often have distorted perceptions of themselves. Everyone has met the woman who thinks she's a caring, compassionate person, but drives everyone crazy with her incessant questions about the smallest details of your life. Or your tour group includes those people who think the fact they paid good money for the trip means they are entitled to the best seats, best views, best rooms, et cetera, and et cetera. The fact everyone else paid the same amount for the trip seems to get overlooked in their desire to have the perfect trip that will be the envy of their friends in the retelling.

When I started to write this book, I was amazed at how many great travel stories revolved around funny people and the circumstances they created. People told me time and time again, it was often the people they met who created the lasting memories they had of a trip. We don't want to be the person guides talk about around the campfire years later, but someone has to take on that role.

Sometimes it's an unexpected set of circumstances that creates this human drama. A wise person once told me that when you squeeze an orange, you get orange juice; and when you squeeze a person out of their comfort zone, you get what is really inside them.

I used to be under the delusion that I was as easy going traveller. Then a brave friend pointed out that, while I have an optimistic nature, I get stressed when things don't go as planned. I've since learned I'm a happier traveller when I've done the research. My itinerary has extra time for unplanned events, and I only trust my safety to travel suppliers who take risk management seriously.

It can be fascinating to observe this process at work in ourselves, and in our travel companions. I think the opportunity to explore our inner frontiers is a big motivator for many travellers, and keeps our suitcases in constant readiness to explore new cultures and our reactions to them.

Based On Double Occupancy

"Travellers never think that THEY are the foreigners." ~ Mason Cooley

While many people want to meet local people, debate has raged in academic circles about whether large numbers of tourists are good for the communities. The people who favor travel often trot out the argument that it allows people to learn about other countries and expand their awareness of their inner selves. Other people argue that most contact between travellers and local people is superficial, and too many travellers in one place can change the host culture. Travellers can demand the changes to meet their requirements, such as when they want to sunbathe topless in conservative Muslim cultures. Other times the changes are more subtle, like when children see and want the clothes or technology that travellers bring with them.

For the most part I agree that travel can provide positive benefits to host communities, and can broaden a traveller's personal horizons. However, there are times when I've wondered about people, the gaps in their knowledge of the world around them and their painful-to-watch contact with local people.

On one of my trips to Africa, I signed up my husband Colin and I with a high-end safari company for a few days of wildlife watching. I knew from personal experience that an African safari at a bargain price could lead to disaster. With more people than windows on cheaper tours, I've ended up with pictures of armpits instead of antelope, and more bruised toes than you'd get waltzing with a gorilla.

Paying extra for a window seat on safari is a wise decision, and you get a chance to enjoy the view and time with your travelling companions, instead of spending time taking someone's elbow out of your ear. On this particular trip, Colin and I were paired up with a young woman from California, Dawn, and a couple from Georgia, Jack and Diane.

Dawn seemed to epitomize a California valley girl, and thought the tour guide was her personal banker, asking him for cash every time she saw a road-side shop she wanted to patronize. Dawn had run out of money on day two, but kept shopping as the company saw fit to advance her more funds. I hope they had done a credit check or had some way to recoup the money.

Jack and Diane seemed like a nice, older couple. With it being the off season, there weren't many people travelling, so there was lots of time to lean more about them. Diane told us her favorite animal was the snow leopard. If fact, she said, she was so fond of the animal that, back home, she had a full length snow leopard fur coat. I could only listen to this in horror! I knew from my zoo training that she was probably wearing five percent of the entire population of the species on her back, and in a place where staying warm wasn't a problem.

Jack had not travelled much, outside of a stint in the military when he was younger. This trip to Africa was a trip of a lifetime for him, and he was so excited he could hardly sit still. He had a very small camera, probably better suited to family Christmas snapshots, but he would excitedly bring it out every few minutes to scan the horizon for the perfect shot.

It was the rainy season and the vegetation was lush and green. Everywhere you looked there were animals, particularly antelope, taking full advantage of the respite from the dry season to eat and reproduce. Our little group seemed to be getting along well, and enjoying the sight of animals all around us.

After shooting his third roll of film, Jack started to ask when we would be seeing tigers. At first I thought he was kidding. When he told us one of his deepest wishes was to see herds of tigers, I knew someone in the van was going to have a disappointing day. Our tour guide seemed to develop sudden hearing loss and never commented on Jack's increasingly frequent laments at the lack of tiger herds on the landscape.

On this particular day, I decided to put my Canadian diplomatic skills to the test. I told Jack as gently as I could that there were no tigers in Africa. I didn't tell him that even if he did go to Asia where tigers are found, there wouldn't be any herds of them. They are solitary creatures and hard to spot at the best of times, but I didn't tell him that. There's a limit to how much bad news a person can take in one day.

At the news, Jack was gob-smacked, as the Newfoundlanders like to say. The surprise then sadness on his face as he digested the fact that would be no tigers on this trip was disheartening to see. He spent the days after that looking out the window complaining that there were no animals. I assumed he meant no animals that he was interested in, as the savannah was covered in wildlife as far as you could see. I marveled at the poise and dignity displayed by the guides as the situation unfolded. Never once did they show any displeasure over Jack's constant criticism of the land they obviously loved so much. And their challenges weren't over.

The last two days of the safari were to be spent at a special tent camp. To stay at the camp we had been asked to pay extra, and select the tent camp option in writing, so there shouldn't have been any surprises when we drove into a camp with tents, but that was not the case. Dawn took one look at her tent and started crying. She wailed that she couldn't possibly sleep in a tent.

I'm not sure what she was expecting when she signed up for the tent camp. These tents even came with flush toilets and hot showers, but she wasn't looking at this stop as a chance to learn more about camping or her personal fortitude. "The animals will eat me," she wailed. No amount of logic or calm assurances from the staff made a difference. Finally, Diane offered to bunk with her and that seemed to be the workable solution. Liberal servings from the bar and some superb southern diplomacy got us through the night.

As the years have passed, I couldn't tell you all the animals I saw that trip, but I will never forget the people I travelled with. It was not the last time I would see how influential travelling companions can be in the success or failure of a trip.

The People You Meet

"There are only two reasons to sit in the back row of an airplane: Either you have diarrhea, or you're anxious to meet people who do." ~ Henry Kissinger

I'm not the only person who thinks one of the best things about travel is the people you meet. Bill Bryan, a cofounder of Off The Beaten Path, a Montana-based adventure tour company, says, "If I ask one of our clients to tell me what the best part of a trip was for them, they'll spend at least half of it describing the people they met, or the adventures they experienced with other people."

Bill is no exception. When he looks back on the many years of leading trips to some of the world's most beautiful places, he quickly remembers the people he met, often before he thinks of the sights he saw.

One year, Bill was leading a tour group to Patagonia in South Argentina and met one of his most memorable travellers, a vibrant woman named Henrietta.

Henrietta was travelling with her partner; and, as Bill found out later, they had had lied about their ages when completing the pre-trip questionnaire. Fearing they might be rejected as being too old for the strenuous trip, they claimed they were 73 and 78. In fact they were much older. "I later found out she was almost 80," Bill says, "and her partner was well over 80."

If you have ever been to Patagonia you might understand why Henrietta and her husband didn't want to miss the chance to see it. Patagonia is found at the southern end of South America and reaches from the Atlantic Ocean to the Pacific, encompassing the Andes Range in both Chile and Argentina. There are five distinct eco-subregions and wildlife watching here is a feast for devoted nature lovers with flamingos, guanacos, and one of the highest concentrations of condors found anywhere.

For hikers, the biggest attractions are the spectacular mountains found in Argentina's Los Glaciares National Park. One of the most visible is the giant Fitz Roy Massif. Fitz Roy was named after the Captain of the Beagle, the ship that carried Charles Darwin around South America in the 1830s. The park itself is 2,300 square miles and includes forests, sheer granite spires, large glaciers and sparkling lakes. Nearby is the spectacular Torres Del Paine National Park. Hiking the trails here is considered one of the great nature treks of the world.

Packing for a trip in Patagonia means you need to bring along protective clothing and lots of layers. The bad weather in Patagonia is legendary and frequent travellers realize a trip can be quickly ruined if you don't bring along the gear needed to stay warm. The fierce winds can feel never-ending; and, in the winter months, hiking conditions are so bad most tour companies avoid the region. But the Patagonia region is a "must-do" for keen adventure travellers, so once the warmer summer months arrive, tour companies head south with their popular hiking tours.

Off The Beaten Path has been taking people to Patagonia for many years. Bill met Henrietta and her husband on a March tour that included a multi-day itinerary of hiking, walking and sightseeing.

One particular morning the group was hiking along a narrow trail enjoying the views and the idle chatter that often springs up as hikers pick their way along a path. Bill was startled out of his reverie by a sudden shriek, rarely a good thing on hiking trips. They are usually harbingers of bad news such as twisted ankles, unexpected wildlife (all of it large or threatening) or lost possessions. This shriek was no exception.

Bill turned quickly to see what had happened, and found himself looking at the small river beside the trail. Henrietta's hat was bobbing on the surface. Henrietta was underneath it. Bill remembers staring in disbelief. "All I could see was her hat sticking out of the water," he said. By bad luck, she had fallen into the only part of the river deep enough to submerge her completely.

Bill and the other hikers scrambled to the water's edge and grabbed Henrietta's arms and whatever part of her pack they could reach. Within seconds they had hoisted her out. Bill said the first thing that came to mind, "You're completely soaked," which was perhaps stating the obvious. Henrietta may have had a different definition of wet as the rest of us. Her reply was, "No, I'm not."

It was likely one of those conversational reflexive responses like when someone asks how you are, and you say you're fine because that is your habit, not because everything is well. In this case, even the best Gore Tex wouldn't have kept Henrietta dry. Everyone has been in a situation where they want to deny misfortune or not inconvenience others, so they hasten to assure everyone they're alright when it's blatantly obvious they're lying or mildly delusional.

Henrietta's brave words didn't hold much sway with Bill. He and the other hikers rallied to help her avoid hypothermia. The women opened their packs and came up with enough clothes to dress Henrietta from head to toe in warm, dry gear. Neither fashionable nor the right size, but it did the job, and the trip continued. Henrietta wasn't any worse for the experience and she proved to be a continuing source of entertainment as the days unfolded, Bill said.

"We ask our guests to fill out a questionnaire before our trips so we can learn more about them and their interests," Bill said, "Henrietta had listed her interests as sex and clowning around!" Most people like to clown around, but Henrietta wasn't kidding. She really was a clown, complete with the costume and the painted face. She would put on her clown outfit and entertain people at hospitals in her community.

Bill got a taste for her clown skills, in particular her knack with balloons. Bill recalls "As we were driving down the road she proceeded to quietly blow up this big, thin balloon which was getting longer and longer. She was sitting behind the bus driver and as the balloon got bigger it started to poke over the bus driver's left shoulder. He was pretty surprised to see a balloon slowly emerge from the passenger seat behind him, and come to rest on his shoulder. But he handled it well. He kept his eyes on the road and Henrietta presented him with a balloon animal once she had twisted and pushed the balloon into a surprisingly realistic rendition of a critter. We all had a good laugh about it," Bill recalls, "and I realized this is why we do lead trips, for the people."

Bill observes, "Patagonia has some of the most beautiful scenery in the world, but it's interesting that when I recall that trip, one of the first things I think about is Henrietta, her spill in the river and her entertaining nature!"

Showing Them The Door

"I have found out that there ain't no surer way to find out whether you like people or hate them than to travel with them." ~ Mark Twain

Bill isn't the only one to discover that some of the funniest travel experiences arise from your choice of travel partners and their actions. John Hull, the Associate Director of the New Zealand Research Institute, remembers one of his funniest travel experiences. He had finished a tourism project on the island of Newfoundland and was driving his rented Buick Cutlass back to his home base in Montreal, Quebec.

John drove his car onto the ferry at Port aux Basques on Newfoundland's southwest coast and parked. This trip can be uncomfortable during rough seas, and at seven hours sailing time, just plain long during good weather. John had invited a coworker named Mary along for the ride. They both had full briefcases and were able to spend much of the voyage catching up on paperwork.

John had noticed that Mary was very proud of her long, curly hair, and she often took a few minutes to comb her locks and fluffing her 'do' so she would look her best. John had found it a distracting habit, but it seemed harmless. Who could have predicted that being preoccupied with your hair-do would lead to unexpected travel consequences?

When the ferry arrived at North Sydney, Nova Scotia, all the passengers with cars had returned to their vehicles, and were waiting for their turn to disembark. Mary got into the car, leaving the passenger door open while she fluffed her hair yet again. Seconds later, a large semi-trailer truck pulled off the ferry in a hurry, ripping the door quickly and cleanly off the car, and sending it flying. The door lay a few feet along the deck, rocking slowly. The window glass was smashed to a million little pieces, and the truck tail lights disappearing in the distance. Apparently the trucker wasn't coming back to discuss liability.

"Can you pick up my door?" John said, only slightly sarcastically. Mary walked over to the door, picked it up and came back to the Buick. "What do you want me to do with this?" she asked.

"Just hold it in place," John said, "We'll go to a garage and see what they can do."

The garage owner was less than optimistic. "We can't fix your door here, but perhaps we could tie it to the car, so you can make it back to Montreal where a body shop can fix it for you," he said. Using some sturdy rope, the mechanic tied the door onto the car so the passenger side was not open to the elements; but the broken window couldn't be covered, as the ropes had to be wrapped around the window frame several times.

"It was a breezy drive," John remembers, "It took us two days to get home and it was pretty awkward for Mary to have to enter and exit the car through the driver's side or crawl through the window. I don't think the constant breeze did much for her hair-do either."

"When we finally got back to Montreal, we parked the car at the office and called the rental company to tell them where to find it," John said, "We told them we'd had a small problem with the door. They almost fell over when they saw the 'small problem', but I didn't much care. I was just glad to finally be home."

This trip didn't stop John from travelling, but he learned "never to travel again with people with high-maintenance hair!"

The Night The Luggage Drowned

"He who would travel happily must travel light." ~ Antoine de Saint-Exupery

We all know when we've been in the company of someone who is described as 'high maintenance'. They often require (or demand) extra care and handling to keep them happy. For some women on the road, this can mean dragging extra suitcases so they always have the right outfit for each occasion, and enough beauty products to look their best, regardless of climate conditions. While I am guilty of dragging hairspray and makeup on most of my travels, I long ago learned that less is more when it comes to luggage.

One of the most unusual situations I found myself in was the result of a high-maintenance woman, travelling the world with more luggage than she could handle. Things came to a climax one stormy night in Greece. The air was still damp from the recent rains that had kept us trapped on the tiny island of Naxos. No ferry had sailed for almost three days because the seas were too high to ensure a safe or comfortable voyage. After sitting far too long in the small cafes along the harbor waiting for the deep bellow of the ship's horn telling us it was once again safe to travel, we were very anxious to leave this tiny, non-descript island.

The travel brochure had promised a lovely fall tour at a reasonable price and the chance to meet other adventure-minded people. So far I had come close to developing hypothermia, chronic boredom as most of the sights were closed for the season; and my roommate, Gloria, had turned out to be a maladjusted psychologist. There had been way too much time for senseless conversation while we had been stranded on Naxos, and I was desperate to move on.

As if to answer my prayers, the sound of the ships horn split the silence. "We must be leaving tonight," Gloria said, "Let's get back to our room and pick up our bags." Our tour leader, Kevin was well organized and I knew he'd be expecting us on the dock in plenty of time to board. I hastily repacked my clothes in my small suitcase.

I subscribe to the packing wisdom that says you shouldn't bring more luggage than you can carry. Gloria subscribed to a different philosophy. She was busy trying to squeeze her makeup and clothing into one of her many bags.

"Are you sure you're going to be able to carry all those bags?" I asked as I surveyed her assortment of luggage. Gloria was on a year-long trip around the world, and apparently wanted to be dressed properly for every climate and every social occasion. I wasn't sure how she got that many suitcases past the airline screening; but, hey, she was young, blonde, pretty and had a practiced routine of looking helpless. I'm guessing that might have helped.

When we gathered up our bags and staggered out the door, I noticed the wind had not abated. It whipped our skirts around our legs, and flung sand and grit in our faces. It was now safe to sail, but it wasn't going to be fun. I was glad I had stocked up on seasickness pills before leaving Athens. We found the rest of our group huddled together on the quay, waiting for our arrival.

There were lots of people jostling to load onto the ferry and Kevin was anxious to get onboard.

"Carol and Gloria! Hurry and get in that line over there. Gloria, you're going to have to do the best you can with your bags," Kevin yelled over the wind. "I won't have a chance to come back and carry some for you." He strode off to deal with some rather vague-sounding official business. Perhaps he didn't want to strain his back, carrying Gloria's bags.

As Gloria and I got to the front of our line, our real adventure begun. To get on the ferry, passengers were expected to walk a very narrow plank several metres over the ocean. There was a rope to hang onto, but it wasn't a very stable structure. The waves crashing below the ramp did nothing to calm our nerves or improve our balance. Walking the plank is an activity best suited to circus performers or pirates, not overloaded tourists.

I let Gloria board ahead of me so I could buffer her from the people who were clamoring to get on and pushing us from behind. I'm not sure I was doing well at running interference, but I had a ringside seat for what came next.

When the ship's steward asked for Gloria's ticket, she shifted one of her suitcases to find it. The bag plopped out from under her arm, bounced off the gangplank and dropped right into the ocean! I watched in horror as the suitcase bobbed in the cold Aegean Sea.

"My suitcase! Oh my God! My suitcase!" Gloria shrieked. Her screams aroused mild interest in the crew, although no one seemed moved to action.

"Kevin, come quickly! Gloria's suitcase has fallen overboard," I called. Kevin did a quick double take at the suitcase bobbing in the water. He sprinted onto the ferry and grabbed one of the crew. They were able to open a large door in the ship's hold that put them just above the water level. A large man with arms the size of small cannons stuck out a long grappling hook, caught the suitcase handle and started to pull.

The rescue was short-lived. When the sailor yarded on the hook, it became obvious that Gloria had overlooked one small detail, the locking of her suitcase. The case snapped open from the strain and, as we watched open-mouthed, the clothes started to float off in the current.

Gloria sobbed into her hanky, "All my clothes are in that suitcase, I'll have nothing to wear!" The sailor, after he quickly pulled the now near-empty suitcase into the ship, was making a valiant effort to rescue her clothes. He grabbed whatever he could see floating near the door, but there wasn't much to salvage. We watched the clothes bob away, and then sink into the ocean. There's a fashion show in Davey Jones' locker.

When no more clothes were visible, the hatch was closed. I told Gloria, "Let's go and see the captain. You'll need to fill out an accident form to claim your insurance, and you'll need the insurance proceeds if you're going to continue your trip clothed." We herded Gloria onto the ship and up to bridge.

Kevin reappeared from the ship's nether regions and gave Gloria a quick rundown on the clothing they had managed to save. Not much. "We got a wool sweater, a silk scarf, a pair of stockings and a pair of shorts," he reported. Not exactly Gloria's idea of cruise wear. "We hung them up in the engine room to dry," he added hopefully, trying to avert another stream of tears.

Gloria sobbed quietly as she went about the business of talking to the captain. It didn't go well. He was reluctant to put anything on paper that might imply the loss was the fault of the ferry company. We had a few hours to kill on the overnight sailing so she continued to lobby her case.

In the meantime, Kevin came back to the rest of the group, having checked on Gloria's clothes which should have been dry by then from the heat of the nearby engines. They were drying quickly, but in an unexpected way. "I went downstairs and I found the crew using the clothes as clean up rags on some equipment!"

It wasn't a moment I'm particularly proud of, but a gurgle of laughter burst from my lips, and several other people started to laugh as well at this absurd turn of events. Kevin continued, "The clothing is dirty, but I think it can be washed. I took what I could find and put it in Gloria's suitcase and we can sort it out later."

We all agreed that we wouldn't pass the latest news onto Gloria, since we didn't want her to feel even worse. Instead we tried to settle down on the hard wooden benches for a few hours sleep before the ferry docked. It wasn't a particularly successful undertaking. "I think I'm going to be sick," Gloria lamented, "What will I do?" We assured her we would give her what clothing we could spare, and that things would look brighter in Santorini, our next destination.

As the sun started to rise, we saw the island come into view and it was time to gather our things. Kevin came back from the hold looking green, but not from seasickness.

"I can't find it," he said with a look of total disbelief, "Gloria's suitcase is gone. Someone stole it!" By this point the fatigue and the absurdity of the situation overruled etiquette and compassion, and we all started to laugh, except Gloria, of course, who burst into tears.

I thought of my mom's expression, 'If she didn't have bad luck, she'd have no luck at all,' and knew it applied to her in this situation.

I got a postcard from Gloria several months later and, amazingly, she went on to have a wonderful trip. She made the best of the opportunity to buy an entirely new wardrobe and also was making many new friends, using her 'worst travel story ever' as an ice breaker.

Life Under A Cargo Bungee

"The whole object of travel is not to set foot on foreign land; it is at last to set foot on one's own country as a foreign land." ~ G.K. Chesterton

Sometimes your travel companions aren't other people. You may find yourself in a situation where your thoughts are all you have to keep you company. This isn't a bad thing; often the chance to reflect on why you have hit the road can yield some surprising insights.

My normal life is busy and heavily scheduled; contrary to the popular myth, being your own boss doesn't leave much time for spontaneity, especially when you are striving to meet the needs of multiple clients. Time spent sitting on an airplane or driving an automobile can appear as idle time at first glance, but often these periods of enforced isolation can yield benefits. With extra time and few distractions, the mind kicks out of auto-pilot or the hamster-in-a-wheel mode, and you start to really notice the world around you.

Don Morberg, an avid motorcyclist, spends many weekends on his Vulcan Drifter exploring the byways and highways of western Canada. He explains how one day at a road block gave him a new perspective on travel:

I have a hard drive full of photographs of me and my motorcycle; but my favorite is printed out and push pinned to the bulletin board in my home office. It was taken in June 2006 on Interstate 90 somewhere east of Gillette, Wyoming. It's high noon in the photo, about 80 degrees Fahrenheit and we had been unceremoniously stopped by a young woman with nice hair, bad teeth and a large 'stop' sign on a pole. She was wearing coveralls rolled to her hips exposing what looked like a bathing suit top.

"Construction ahead," she said. "There'll be a pilot car here in a minute; she'll lead you." This was the memorized part of the speech. Then she added, "You guys are the coolest looking bikers I seen all day."

"No other traffic eh?" I said, hitting the kill switch and letting silence settle like the dust around me. I could hear music coming from a pile of personal effects in the ditch. My riding companion, known as Sagebrush to all but his intimates, had already shut down and was off his bike, stretching the tin knee he received last autumn courtesy of the Canadian medical system.

"No, it's been busy," she said, not getting it. "Lotta cars, motor homes. Busy all day. In fact, I had to pee and the cars kept coming and coming. I thought I was going to bust."

This was way more than I wanted to know about her, but I nodded sympathetically and looked around. If you ignored the narrow strip of broken up interstate, the entire 360-degree landscape was a series of low, rolling, putty-colored hills, dotted here and there by some scrub brush. There would be nowhere for a modest flag person to relieve herself.

"Are we in South Dakota yet?" I asked. The young woman pointed to the southeastern horizon and smiled. "Almost," she said. "See those black hills? Those are the Black Hills." Her smile drained as a line of cars rolled up behind us. 'Be right back," she said and we never saw her again.

This trip is a long one, the longest I'd ever done. Yesterday, we left Calgary at the crack of dawn; and, 860 kilometres later, I'd collapsed onto a bed at the Holiday Inn Express in Billings, Montana. That was eight hours of riding plus stops for food, gas and, unlike our flag person, washrooms with doors. Today was the short leg; 560 kilometres from Billings to the Black Hills of South Dakota where a couple hundred members of an Internet-based motorcycle group were gathering from all over the continent for a rally. There's another rally in that area in August with half a million bikes; this isn't that one.

At that moment, the music from the ditch was replaced by the hammering of a stuck CD player. It sounded bad enough to be a club dance mix. Sagebrush looked in the direction of the flag girl. She was telling the bad news to the growing line of cars behind us, approaching each one individually, probably saying, "You're the coolest looking car driver I seen all day." Sagebrush walked over to the CD player, poked it and all went strangely quiet.

Quiet was welcome. When you ride long distance on a motorcycle, noise is your constant companion. There's the obvious one, the pounding of the exhaust that everyone thinks of when the word 'motorcycle' is mentioned. Once you've settled into a ride and your bum has become comfortably numb, you notice mechanical noises like the valves, the timing chain, the clutch plates, the transmission gears, the final drive. You get used to their sound and any variation, any tick or clink, catches your attention like a flat clarinet note at the symphony. Then there is the flap, rattle and buzz of various vibrating bike parts. Could be bolts loosening, could be nothing. I like the sounds of tires on different pavement; the hiss of oily blacktop, a deathtrap when it first rains; the grind of flush coating, eating tires like they were Tim Horton doughnuts; the pebbly whine of concrete.

The overwhelming sound, however, is wind. It whistles through the nooks and crannies on the bike, and screams through the flaps and vents in your helmet. It roars against the leather of your jacket, chaps and boots, pressing them against your body. You're the centre of a constant bubble of white noise; but, at some point in the trip, you realize you're moving ahead of it. That's when you're really riding.

It's getting hot in the Wyoming noon sun and there's no sign of the pilot car. I perch my bug-smeared Red Baron goggles on the peak of my once-owned-by-a-California-Highway-Patrol-officer helmet, and unzip my riding jacket. All my worldly requirements for the next two weeks are bungee-corded to the back of the bike with a red elastic cargo net, the greatest invention since duct tape. If they had caught King Kong in one of these things, he'd still be on display at the Central Park zoo. I yank my bottle of Gatorade out from under the elastic, take a swig and swish it around in my mouth. It's my drink of choice on the road; tastes no worse warm than cold.

Sagebrush is walking back from dispatching the CD player and I toss him my digital camera. "Would you get a shot of me with the Black Hills in the background?" He nods. He's an impatient rider and having to stand by the side of the road is frustrating him.

He raises the camera as I stuff the Gatorade bottle back under the elastic cords. I drape my hand casually over the handlebars of the bike; but, as I start to smile, he's already lowering the camera. He hands it to me as he walks past and I put it back into the holster slung at my hip, the way General Custer or Wild Bill Hickock would have tucked away their Colt pistols here 140 years ago.

It dawns on me that today's ride from Billings was a trip through U.S. History. This road took us over the Missouri River, near Fort Benton, past the Lewis & Clark National Forest, within sight of Yellowstone, through the Crow Indian Reservation, past Little Bighorn and near the Northern Cheyenne Reservation. A sign pointed the way to Hole In The

Wall where Jesse James, the Logan brothers, George 'Flat Nose' Currie and Butch Cassidy's Wild Bunch hung out, luckily not all at the same time. Another sign points to Devil's Tower. Ahead of us is Deadwood, Mount Rushmore, Crazy Horse Memorial, Wounded Knee and the geographic centre of the United States. Most of what Americans think of as 'the old west' actually happened in the centre. Custer and Hickock both met their sad ends here in 1876, five weeks apart.

I glugged more Gatorade and squinted out at the heat waves starting to fuzz the horizons. I tried to imagine millions of buffalo moving across the terrain like lava. Somewhere in my saddlebag, I had a map. I had consulted it this morning while eating my "free continental breakfast" muffin to confirm this road would take me to my destination. Now, here on the side of I-90, I realized that arriving at my destination is not nearly as important as I had thought it was when I started this journey. I decided that if I just generally travelled in a southeasterly direction, I would eventually get to where I was going.

Someone once told me, "Young bikers need a destination; old bikers just need a direction." I never really understood it until that moment. I had 1,300 kilometres behind me on this trip; but when I looked back up the highway, I knew much of that was lost opportunity, vanished behind me in blur and noise. My focus had been on the destination and now I realized that was wrong.

Someone honked. Another young woman had arrived. She was in a pickup truck and leading a long line of sweltering cars, trucks and motor homes. She pulled a U-turn and backed up to us. When the line had passed, she signaled us to follow her. We buckled on our helmets, fired up the bikes and did so.

Half an hour later, back on good road, we rolled through a windy, dusty, down-on-its-luck little town called Upton. Outside of a roadside restaurant, a hand-painted sign read, "Welcome to the Upton Testical Festival" (their spelling.) Something written underneath referred to Prairie Oysters. I signaled Sagebrush to pull over. When he looked at me puzzled, I nodded at the sign and said, "Let's check this out."

Ghost Stories

"Somebody told me it was frightening how much topsoil we are losing each year, but I told that story around the campfire and nobody got scared." ~ Jack Handey

As I mentioned earlier, most people like to meet new people on their trips. But what happens when the people they meet are not the flesh and bone kind of person? Kids at camp like to sit around a campfire and tell ghost stories, but few people set out on a trip deliberately looking for ghostly encounters.

Hope Bishop is a traveller who met a very unusual person on one of her trips. In September 2006, she was attending a conference in Salt Lake City. With so many people in town, Hope felt fortunate to have found a hotel room near the convention center. The reservation was at the quaint Peery Hotel. Built in 1910 to house miners, its carefully maintained Victorian décor and small size gives it a charm all its own. There are no mini-bars, only a functional ice machine is found at the end of the hall; and with only three stories it is often faster to climb the stairs than wait for the sedate and rather noisy elevator.

Hope arrived at the Peery to find the reservations for herself, her brother and sister had been mishandled. The rooms they had booked weren't available. The front desk clerk offered them two larger suites on the third floor as a complimentary upgrade. No traveller could refuse the chance for more space at no extra cost, so they took the rooms and filled out the registration forms. Hope and her brother Reid were assigned Room 323, while her sister Nancy and her friend got the suite across the hall.

"We headed up to our rooms," Hope remembers, "We got off this elevator which grunted and groaned as if it wasn't going to make the journey and stopped dead." Hope gazed down the narrow hallway thinking she'd seen this something like this before. She turned to Reid and asked him, "What does this look like? I think it looks just like a scene out of The Shining!" Reid looked startled, and while he didn't disagree. He told her, "Stop talking like that!"

Reid and Hope walked to their room and opened the door, hoping the suite was a nice one. A quick scan of the room showed a couch with a fold out bed and a full bedroom. "I'll flip you for the bedroom," Hope said. It was her lucky day and she found herself with a comfy bed in the Victorian-style bedroom. Reid was a good sport and settled down for the night on the fold-out bed.

Hope was in the middle of a fitful sleep when Reid shook her awake.

"Did you see that woman?" he asked, his eyes looking around the room rapidly, "There was a woman standing at the end of the bed, looking at me; and she's gone. I was dreaming about a woman and when I opened my eyes, there was a young woman standing at the foot of the bed looking at me. I've looked everywhere, but there is no one here."

Hope hadn't been sleeping well herself, but no ghostly apparitions had surfaced in her room. She told Reid "Go back to sleep; you're just been having a bad dream."

The next morning Hope, Reid and Nancy were mingling with some other conference attendees over coffee. Figuring there is nothing like a good ghost story to get the conversation going, Reid told his Nancy about the woman he had seen in the middle of the night. Not a sympathetic audience, she exclaimed, "You're a fruitcake!"

An engineer visiting from England asked Reid what hotel he was staying at. When he heard it was the Peery Hotel, he replied, "Oh, you're on the floor with the ghost. We did some research before we came and the Peery is a haunted hotel."

Hope was shocked to hear that she might be staying in a hotel with people who could walk unannounced through the walls, and decided to quiz the front desk staff.

"Is this hotel haunted?" Hope asked the front desk clerk in what she hoped was a conversational tone.

"Why do you ask?" the young woman replied nervously. Hope explained how her brother had been awoken by a vision of a young woman, and he was convinced it wasn't a dream.

"What room are you staying in?" asked the front desk clerk.

"Room 323," Hope replied.

There is probably no section in the customer service training manual on how to break the news to a guest that they are rooming with a ghost. The clerk gulped and came clean, "Usually she is in room 347 down the hall."

Hope wasn't particularly disturbed by the news. Her brother had already met the ghost and she didn't seem to be intent on harming anyone.

Nancy was as intrigued as Hope by the thought of a ghost living among them, and got the chance to tell other guests about the hotel's unique features later that evening. Two men at the conference had complained about their room at the Peery, and had been moved to another room, on the third floor.

Nancy came across them as they were going into their room and asked, "Do you know you're staying on the floor with the ghost?" Before they could answer a book fell off the shelf behind them, narrowly missing the phone in its downward spiral. Thinking this might not be a coincidence, Hope and Nancy started to ask other guests for more information on the ghost.

A woman from Sacramento complained that she had come back to her room to find all the drawers open. She had thought she'd been the victim of a break and enter, but when she looked more carefully, none of her possessions had been disturbed.

Another person told Hope that more than one guest had checked out of the Peery in the middle of the night because the sheets would suddenly be pulled away from them in their beds. "I imagine it would be a bit of surprise to be sleeping and then suddenly no sheets, and no sign of anyone around to pull them off," Hope commented.

A cleaning woman who has worked in the hotel for over twenty years, told Hope "I often feel someone tapping me on the shoulder and when I turn around there is no one there." She must have nerves of steel or really enjoys paranormal phenomena. Most people would find a hotel sans ghosts for which to work.

With a little research, Hope discovered that a young woman named Mabel was murdered in the hotel in the early 1900s. Mabel had been a prostitute working for the successful miners who frequented the Peery. Hope did not see Mabel herself, but she wasn't surprised by all the unusual activity.

"I learned on that trip to trust my intuition," she says, "When I first saw the third floor and felt like I was in the middle of a horror movie; I should not have been surprised that odd events occurred."

Hope has told many people about her visit to the Peery Hotel, and what surprises her is how often someone has their own ghost story to tell. "I think there are things we can't explain or see in our normal, rational view of the world," Hope concluded, "but my visit to the Peery convinced me that there are spirits from other dimensions influencing events in our lives."

The Sorcerer's Spell

"Finland has long been a popular destination with travelers who enjoy the feeling of knowing that if their car breaks down, they could be eaten by wolves." ~ Dave Barry

I had my own encounter with the supernatural on a trip I did to Iceland. As an expert in ecotourism business development, I'm often invited to lead workshops for people wanting to improve the success of their tourism organizations. Usually, I learn as much as I teach at these events.

In May of 2006, I was visiting northwest Iceland to work with a group of tourism professionals from several Nordic countries. In addition to time in the classroom, we hit the roads of rural Iceland to learn firsthand about traditional lifestyles and the changes tourism is bringing to small communities.

A new venture for the town of Hólmavik is the Museum of Icelandic Sorcery and Witchcraft. Iceland has a long history of story telling and a fascination with magic. Within ten minutes of landing at the international airport outside of Keflavik, I saw souvenirs celebrating the mischievous doings of the Yule lads of Icelandic folklore.

The Icelandic sagas are fables known the world over, and every Icelander will tell you about the 'little people'. These aren't their children they are talking about; these are the really little people who are believed to live under rocks and create magic. Icelanders are extremely practical, industrial people, so it is an amazing contrast when you learn about the magic, storytelling and legends that are a large part of their culture.

The sorcery museum is a relatively new attraction, created to share the history and beliefs around sorcery in Iceland. It is located in the west fjords. If you look at the Iceland map, the west fjords looks like a thumb sticking out from the rest of the country with only a narrow connection to keep it from floating away into the north Atlantic.

As our bus lumbered over the small narrow roads, our guide told us a story about the sorcerers and the black plague in the Middle Ages. Legend has it that several sorcerers sat on the edge of the west fjords and cast spells to keep the black plague from crossing into the region from the rest of the country. The plague never made it to the west fjords. Cynics might argue that the fact there were very few people in this remote area, might account for the lack of disease; but it makes a much better story if you believe the sorcerer's tale.

So, justly primed, we were looking forward to learning more about the magic of Iceland; but first on the agenda was dinner. I sat next to the museum curator at dinner. He could have easily passed for an accountant; neat and tidy with nary an eye of newt to be seen. After a nice meal and a couple of drinks to loosen our cynicism, we left to visit the museum. The curator had gone ahead to open the museum and get ready for our visit.

As we entered the sorcery museum, the curator greeted us, but he was transformed. At dinner he looked like an accountant, but when he greeted us, he was clad in animal skins, and wore a ceremonial wooden head piece with a carved symbol. One of the Icelanders in my group whispered to me that some people believed he really did have special powers.

After an informative tour of the museum's main exhibits, the curator took us into the main exhibit hall. He explained that he had a problem and needed our help. He said that a rather nasty spirit was scaring the villagers and, with the full moon rising, he needed our help to cast a spell that would drive the creature away.

As dinner theater goes, I could tell this was going to be pretty spectacular. He gave us each a rock with a heliographic character painted on it; saying he created it with the blood of his mother's first menstrual period. He looked to be about fifty, but it seemed rude to ask him how one stores blood for that length of time. I assumed it was part of the show and waited eagerly for the rest to unfold.

I wasn't disappointed. We held our rocks and joined hands in a large circle. Our curator delivered an impressive performance, shouting traditional verses and ringing a bell that gave his words extra drama. No one said a word, and I actually could feel a special energy in the room. It could have been the result of too many people for too small a room, but I preferred to think it was something more.

When we finished casting the spell, he told us to keep our rocks with us. He said they would keep us safe while we in the west fjords, but under NO circumstances were we take the rock out of Iceland, or the bad spirits would follow us home and give us many sleepless nights. Now, in addition to keeping track of my passport and other valuables, I had a small, bloody rock that I couldn't lose. I slipped it into my pocket, and didn't think about it until the next day.

The next morning dawned with beautiful sunny skies. We were scheduled to visit the nearby Grimsey Island, renowned for its large colonies of puffins. I was very excited about the possibility of seeing puffins. Every time I had visited a destination to see puffins, they had left before I arrived.

The puffins near our hotel in Dangnes were still in the area, but the winds had been blowing at gale force levels for several days. The ship's captain had earlier said he wasn't sure we would be able to make the trip, but now the fjord was like glass. We loaded the bus and headed for the harbor.

The bus wound down a narrow road that is typical of rural Iceland; the views of the ocean and the barren hills were spellbinding. Suddenly, a large sea eagle swooped down to almost bus level. It flew alongside the bus for several minutes, almost like an aerial escort to the harbor. It gave us great photo opportunities and we were pumped for our puffin viewing.

There was some jostling as we piled onto the boat that would take us to the puffin island. It was a fishing boat, not something set up for tourists, and seating was limited. Trying not to trip over the various ropes on deck and pitch myself into the ocean, I leaned against the rail next to a retired Norwegian sea captain.

He had a ready laugh and an interesting blend of cynicism and superstition. After chiding me for bringing a back pack on board, which sailors believe is bad luck, he turned his attention to the water.

"Look at that," he said as he pointed to the ocean, "It's smooth as glass and last night it was so rough we thought we would be canceling our trip. It isn't natural." I was just glad we were going, and didn't give much thought to possible supernatural interventions.

With our binoculars trained on the puffins and other birds swimming near the boat, time passed quickly. We reached the island quickly and offloaded on the makeshift landing dock. Some might call have called it a large log, not a dock; but we managed to get to shore with dry feet.

The island was uninhabited, and while it appeared small from the water, it became a lot larger when we started walking over its slopes. We climbed a steep trail to reach the highest point. For most of the shoreline, the island cliffs towered over the surrounding seas, making it an ideal nesting site for the puffins.

In a move not sanctioned by any insurance company, we lay on our bellies and shimmied to the edge of the cliffs to look down, way down at the puffins. If a person was to fall off the cliff, it would no doubt be a very bad thing, but at that time, our biggest fear was puffin fleas which hang out around the birds' nests. I hadn't realized there was such a creature, but I figured it would make a great story at the medical clinic if I happened to pick up a few! "Yes, I have puffin fleas. Do you have a salve for that?" Perhaps it would even score me extra space on the plane home. After all who wants to ride next to a possible flea host?

All too soon our puffin watching time was up, and we headed across the island to meet the waiting boat. We picked our way over the rocks and climbed aboard to share stories while we waited to push off. And we waited and waited. All but two people were accounted for. Several people went back on foot to search for the missing members of our group, while a small fishing boat started to circle the island to search from the water.

We thought of the steep cliffs on the island, and hoped no one had come to an unfortunate end. After much waiting and worrying, the missing people were found on a remote slope, looking frantically for the boat.

We were quickly reunited and the ship's captain headed the boat for home. Our tour leader asked suddenly, "How many of you brought your rocks from last night?" Everyone put up their hands except for the two people who had been lost. We all laughed, but was it a coincidence?

"Look at that," my grizzled sea captain friend said, pointing to the sudden increase in waves. "The wind picked up again as soon as we left the island. Maybe there is something to that sorcery business after all."

Sometimes You Shouldn't Ask

"Travel and change of place impart new vigor to the mind." ~ Seneca

Local color is often charming; and the unique customs, food and business practices of a region help it stand out from other destinations. Advertising campaigns will often pick up on a charming feature of a city or country and use it to attract tourists. However, there are times when the local color can detract from a trip.

There are things that you do not want to know. It can ruin what otherwise might be a good travel day. The old adage "ignorance is bliss" means you can delude yourself into thinking your hotel is well run or that the tour company knows what they are doing. I try not to linger in blissful ignorance too long, but sometimes I'm not always ready for the answers I get when I dig deeper.

I was visiting the famous Mt. Kenya Safari Club and the woman at the front desk told me I could go horse back riding while my husband tried out the golf course. This was not your typical safari stop; the luxurious trappings and protocol overwhelmed the wildlife watching.

"You can't leave your room after 6 p.m. unless you are wearing a suit jacket," our hostess warned my husband.

"Not my idea of a good evening," he muttered, but he was going to make the most of the daylight hours by hitting the links while I was going riding in the African bush.

At the stables, I met the trail guide and was given a horse and a helmet. I launched myself up onto the big Bay's back and realized the small English saddle had very little to hang onto. I was used to a Western saddle which seemed almost like an easy chair compared to this small slab of leather.

The ride would last about an hour; and, after a few rules about staying in line and not racing the horses, we set off for the forest. The recent heavy rains made the steep trail muddy. My horse slipped and stumbled, searching for his footing. He didn't seem to have the surefootedness I was used to when riding through the Canadian mountains. I was getting increasingly worried.

"Where do you get your horses from?" I asked our guide.

"The racetrack," he said. "These are thoroughbreds that can't run on the track anymore." If I would have stopped talking there, I might have had a relaxed ride; but no, I had to probe deeper. "How do you train these horses for trail riding?" I said.

"Humph, no training is needed. We just cut down on their oats," my guide said.

Here I'd been spending months and years at home training my horse to respond to commands, and all the while I had been wasting my time. Just cut down on the oats to make them quieter and you'll have a horse suitable for something they've never been trained to do. I thought, "Right!"

I was not sure if I should ask for more details about their horse training methods, but I was not able to relax with the information he had shared so far. We were riding across wild landscapes with buffalo, elephant, wildebeest and zebra. What if the horse wasn't the right temperament for trail riding among the wild animals of Africa? I could only hope my race horse would keep his head and his rider (me), if something startled him. Would he revert to his racetrack beginnings? I had no aspirations to ride Kentucky Derby-style amongst wild animals that could hurt me.

Although I got out of that one unscathed, it wasn't the only time I discovered information that did not add to travel enjoyment.

I was staying in a large hi-rise hotel in Fort Myers, Florida, for a conference. On the surface it appeared to be a nice property; large rooms, a beautiful pool and good meeting facilities. I had heard mutterings that the conference organizers had found the hotel manager difficult to deal with, often cutting corners without considering the effect on us, the conference attendees.

One conference goer, Bob, had us in stitches when he told us about his first afternoon at the hotel. He had been working in his room when the fire alarm sounded. Normally a fire alarm in a hotel is a false alarm, and most people will look around or wait for further instructions before evacuating, especially when it means a long walk down several flights of stairs.

Bob opened his door when he first heard the alarm to see if it was for real. What he saw had him heading for the exits, pronto.

"The housekeeping staff was running as fast as they could for the exits. I decided this was no false alarm and followed them at a trot," he said. It turned out to be a false alarm, but we all agreed it was very unusual for people to get that excited about a fire alarm in the absence of smoke or fire.

I was telling this story to my taxi driver as I left for the airport. He laughed and said, "The fire department usually keeps a truck nearby and has one eye on that building. They think the owner wants to burn it down to collect the insurance!" I guess this rumor was well known and the staff wasn't taking any chances on getting caught in a fire.

I felt lucky I hadn't ended up on the evening news as a displaced fire victim. It was another trip that would have been better if I hadn't known about the local rumors.

Get Stuffed!

"Travel becomes a strategy for accumulating photographs." ~ Susan Sontag

Some of best places to visit are not the big tourism attractions, but those communities with unique or unusual attractions.

I'm always delighted when I come across a local treasure; something so different you lose track of time as you explore. Ideas can be easily copied so it's a treat to find a truly original tourism concept. I think the most successful attractions reflect the community's character in a way that engages the visitor.

That's why I had wanted to visit the world-famous Gopher Hole Museum in Torrington, Alberta, for many years. I finally found a free weekend and managed to guilt my husband Colin into making the trip. I said he would get a few million husband points for giving up a hike in the mountains; plus he'd be the envy of all his coworkers who spent their weekend just camping or doing something else normal.

Most people have never heard of the world famous Gopher Hole Museum, and couldn't find it on a map if they tried. It's located about an hour and a half northeast of Calgary in the middle of the short grass prairie. The village of Torrington boasts a few hundred residents and does have not much in the way of natural tourism attractions.

Legend has it that some people wanted to bolster the local economy by getting more tourists to visit. Realizing they did not have much to work with, they got creative. One of the local women was a doll collector, and thought perhaps a museum with a unique collection would be a good idea. But what could they put in the museum? The one thing Torrington has in abundance is gophers, properly known as the Richardson's ground squirrel.

Gophers are a pest to farmers and ranchers. Livestock can trip in the gopher holes and break limbs, so often the rodents are exterminated. Take some expired gophers and stuff them for the museum display. Volunteers would make costumes for the gophers, and they would be displayed in dioramas that would depict everyday life in a prairie town.

I was expecting something fairly hokey at the museum and wasn't disappointed. I yanked open the door, skipped the entrance desk, and was smack dab in the middle of stuffed gophers. The room was dark except for the lights that shone out of the little brown boxes, each of them a separate display.

Everywhere there were scenes of gophers in action, I couldn't decide where to look first. A gopher with wings caught my eye, so I took a sharp left to find myself looking at a church scene. A gopher was dressed in clergy robes and posed as if giving a sermon. I thought the flying angel gopher over his left shoulder was a nice touch, and burst out laughing when I noticed a gopher posed in the corner, asleep in a church pew. Everyone has probably felt like that gopher at one time or another; I mean the tired part, not the stuffed part. I could tell the people behind this museum had a rich sense of humor.

Colin had gotten into the spirit of the museum, and pulled me over to look at the Olympic scene. The painted backdrop showed many different gopher families sitting on blankets in the grass, watching the winners of the Gopher Olympics take the podium for their medals. The games had been altered to fit the gopher theme. The winners were wearing ribbons demonstrating their prowess in such noted feats as "Best Car Dodger," something that gophers don't always excel at.

Each of the displays was cleverly crafted. One of the scenes poked fun at the complaints they had received from animal activists. A hippy-looking gopher with a black beard and a poncho was demonstrating against one of the town fathers, also a gopher. The protest sign said "G.A.G.S. - gophers against getting stuffed."

Other displays had a prehistoric gopher, a testament to the early history of Torrington, and a curling scene celebrated one of Canada's most popular winter activities. The gopher lying on the ice after throwing his curling rock reminded me of my attempts to play, and I laughed. I noticed the other people visiting the museum were also enjoying a chuckle or two.

This unusual wildlife attraction is entertaining in ways I had never imagined. The museum is run by community volunteers so their operating budget is tiny, but they've received media coverage all over the world. No doubt this is too good, or bizarre, a story to pass up. Even the National Enquirer did a story on the museum.

About 6,000 people come to the Gopher Hole Museum each year. Some buy the certificates that testify to their visit at the quirky attraction, others just pay their $2 admission. The money raised goes toward several community projects and the volunteer fire department. It definitely gets my vote for most unusual wildlife watching destination and it seems to be very community based. I left feeling with a better understanding of small town prairie life.

Lost In Eastern Alberta

"Thanks to the Interstate Highway System, it is now possible to travel from coast to coast without seeing anything." ~ *Clifton Fadiman*

As I found in Torrington, many people would agree that the best travel experiences come from small, out-of-the way discoveries, the things that might not make the travel brochures. It might be the chance to try out someone else's lifestyle, or to make new friends through shared laughs over minor misfortunes.

I love my work as a tourism consultant because I get the chance to visit small communities before they have been discovered by mainstream tourists. Often they have few tourism facilities and any they do have are created and run by volunteers. Touring these places, you need to ask a few more questions to unearth the sites worth seeing. Usually it helps to have extra snacks, libations or reading material on hand in the event of a quiet evening.

A couple of years ago I was working with some people from the communities in east central Alberta to develop a tourism plan. The towns of Oyen and Consort are the main centers in this sparsely-populated part of the province. They aren't big. The population of the total area is only 12,000 people spread over a region of roughly 20,000 square kilometres.

The region received a 'special areas' designation because the land and living conditions there are much different than anywhere else in the province. This land is part of the Palliser Triangle, better as rangeland than farmland. In an effort to settle the west, the government encouraged farmers to break the land. It was an economic and environmental disaster. The land would not support grain crops, and many families suffered extreme hardships, fighting for survival.

The Alberta Economic Development department wanted to create a tourism link between the communities there and those in central and southern Alberta that shared common geography, culture and history. The project was intended to create a major new tourism destination, The Canadian Badlands. It would showcase the agricultural, paleontological, cultural and natural experiences in this region of understated beauty and ruggedness.

One of the occupational hazards of a project like this is that the travel is done in the off season, leaving me to imagine leaves on the trees, birds in the bushes and people in the shops. Many of the attractions were closed, and blizzards and snowfalls made the roads hazardous.

As I did my background research for the project, I came to the conclusion this area was a bit of a black hole for tourism.

I was working with John, the car door-less consultant from Montreal on his first trip to Alberta. John and I hit the roads one sunny January afternoon for our first site visit in the area. I had loaded up the 4 X 4 with winter emergency supplies, laptops and snacks for the trip. I told John about the history of the prairies as we drove and tossed around ideas for the project.

We travelled through the spectacular Red Deer River valley, briefly admiring the hoodoos before we turned east. We still had another two hours of driving and the days were short. Past Drumheller, we headed into lands less travelled. The farms along the road became less and less frequent. Even the fences that usually line the highways eventually ran out as there were no farm animals to keep off the road. The telephone poles even seemed to be fewer and fewer.

I had grown up on the prairies, and yet I had not experienced this type of landscape. It was wide open, and empty of any signs of civilization. But there were compensations. I was thrilled to see the occasional snowy owl perched on a fence post and we even encountered large herds of antelope. These animals are the second fastest land animals after cheetahs, and it was a thrill to watch them as they ran off in a blur. It made me feel I was back in Africa on safari.

We passed some small bed-and-breakfasts, all with No Vacancy signs on the road. Oil and gas exploration was booming, and most people staying here were on business.

John and I followed our map to the largest hotel in the area. Not very big by big city standards, it had about twenty rooms on two floors. The parking lot was full of large half-ton trucks sporting logos of construction or oil and gas companies. We'd been warned that it might not have the charm we were expecting so we made our way to our rooms with some trepidation.

My room was fairly modern with a few dozen stations on the TV for entertainment, and was on the bottom floor, actually the basement. I opened the blinds to discover my window looked up at the radiators of about a half a dozen large trucks. I decided the closed curtains would be a better scenic choice. John came over to see how I was faring. His room had a shower with a view. In it, he could see light from the floor above him. He expressed concern that his ceiling, someone else's floor, might totally give way and collapse on top of him.

"It's only for one night," I told him. We made it a practice on these projects to stay in as many different places as possible to could get a feel for the area, and see what types of service tourists could expect. The next night we would be staying at a small B&B which promised rural charm and a quiet getaway.

In small communities where hotels are scarce, farmers and ranchers will sometimes set up B&Bs to supplement their incomes. Most of them are quite charming and well run, but not marked or marketed as well as they could be.

When I had called to reserve at the B&B, I had written down the directions carefully. We would be in meetings until well after dark, and I feared signs might be scarce. I didn't know how true that would be until we attempted to find the place.

John and I had enjoyed supper at a small restaurant in Consort. One thing about small towns, you lose your anonymity. People notice you're new in town and you're something to talk about.

We headed out of town following the instructions I'd memorized: "Look for a sign on the left which will tell us where to turn off the highway," It was one of those crystal clear nights you get during a cold, prairie winter. There was almost no traffic, so we could slow down and look for our sign. We never found it.

I was clocking off the kilometres on the odometer and it was obvious we had missed the turnoff.

We had been paying close attention to the road so I didn't know how that was possible. We did a U-turn and retraced our route. Still no sign.

We flipped open our cell phones to call for further directions, and discovered we were out of cell phone range. "This is the kind of remote place where people spot flying saucers and aliens," I joked to John.

He laughed and said, "That would be an interesting angle to our tourism plan."

We scanned the horizon and saw...nothing. No lights, no signs of life except for the darkened tarmac that stretched out beyond our high beams. I drove towards Oyen, hoping to pick up a cell phone signal. Eventually we did, but it was getting late. We decided it would be better to find a room than spend more time looking for our turnoff.

We knew where there would be a room. I called last night's hotel to see if they had rooms available. Perhaps John could get his shower with a view again.

"You're supposed to be at the B&B tonight," the desk clerk told me when I gave her my name. "We have no secrets," I whispered to John.

I explained to the hotel clerk that it was late, we were lost and we would really like to come in from the cold. I couldn't remember having to justify my need for a room before but I was ready to do just about anything to get off the road and call it a day. I guess we passed inspection because we got our rooms. I called the B&B to apologize for our inability to find them. I promised we would try harder next time.

And we did. For our next attempt to find the B&B, I took copious notes including the mileage from all major landmarks, major being a relative word in this part of the world. It was again dark when John and I turned down Highway 41, determined to find the B&B. It had become a matter of professional pride that we find this place. Both of us had geography degrees and had travelled far too much to be thwarted by something that was supposed to be located so close to the road.

As we counted off the kilometres, we came to a turnoff, a small gravel road. It didn't really look like a road and there was no sign visible. There had been some suspicious reflective tape further back in the ditch so I backed the car up and turned on the high beams. Sure enough, it was the sign for the B&B, about the size of a dinner plate.

"No wonder we missed it," I muttered, "You probably couldn't see that in broad daylight."

The gravel road off the highway was ice covered and none too wide. I was blessing my decision to buy a 4X4.

"I'd never drive a road this rutted and deserted at night by myself," I told John. In the dark it looked like one of those empty roads that people get stuck on, and find themselves eating the soles of their shoes before they are rescued days or weeks later.

Not wanting to miss the driveway for the B&B, we crept along the road. As I peered over the dashboard something on the road ahead looked particularly 'fluffy'. I figured either an animal or an alien was laying there, so I slowed even more. In the high beams, I could finally make out the mysterious creature. "It's a porcupine!" I said. It was coming straight at us in the middle of the road.

We stopped and the prickly creature detoured around us. The moon was rising now and, with the landscape awash in a cool white light, it was easier now to see the road. That was unfortunate since I could now see there was a lot more ice than I had initially thought. I was concentrating on not sliding into the ditch when a large owl suddenly swooped across the road and a few metres later, a deer looked up, grazing in the bushes next to the road.

I was trying to remember if Aboriginals considered an owl an omen of impeding death or good luck, while I clocked off the remaining kilometres. "This travel business is a glamorous life, isn't it?" I asked John.

Finally, the lights of a farmyard came into view. There was a small house with the B&B sign on it, but it looked deserted. A woman watched us through the window of the more-modern home across the yard. In an odd move for someone in the hospitality business, she darted out of sight when we got out of the car. "Maybe she's shy," John said.

We were relieved when we knocked and the door swung open. A friendly face greeted us. "You'll be in the building you just drove by. What time would you like breakfast?" she asked.

We quickly negotiated a time, and headed to our rooms. The house was full of comfortable ranch furniture, antiques and crafts. The Winter Olympics were on the TV, courtesy of a satellite link-up; and suddenly all felt right with the world again.

"I'll toss you for the Lazy Boy," I told John and settled in to watch some world-class curling.

Diary Of An Urban Musher

"I think that travel comes from some deep urge to see the world, like the urge that brings up a worm in an Irish bog to see the moon when it is full." ~ Lord Dunsany

I told you earlier about my dog sled driving adventures, but that wasn't my first time looking at the back ends of sled dogs.

I grew up in Saskatchewan, and, when I was young, I never really thought it was much of a tourism destination. I was always looking west to the mountains as a better place to spend summer holidays. Now that I now longer live in Saskatchewan, I look at it with different eyes. It will always be my homeland, but I can now see the understated beauty of its open spaces, and living skies; the slogan now found on its license plates. The people here are my people, the type you often hear referred to as "the salt of the earth".

I am proud to know the small group of tourism professionals who have struggled with limited resources to build the Saskatchewan Nature and Ecotourism Association. The task they have undertaken would overwhelm a much bigger organization, but with that can-do attitude often displayed by westerners, they have created a splash in the world of nature tourism.

In the late 1990s, I was invited to speak at a workshop organized by a Society board member at Anglin Lake in northern Saskatchewan. I would be speaking the day before a dogsled operator would share his experiences in setting up a touring company. His talk would be followed by the chance for all of us to go dog sledding. I had always wanted to try dog sledding and this was my first chance to do so.

The next morning, I put on a layer of long underwear followed by a layer of fleece, then a windbreaker, then I threw on another fleece top just to be safe. Then I started with the 'serious' outdoor clothes: snow pants, down parka, neck gaiter, headband, down mitts, two pairs of socks and Sorel boots.

Looking like a hopeful applicant for a Pillsbury Doughboy commercial, I drove over to the main lodge, arriving before the workshop participants and the mushers – Brad and his partner Susan of SunDog Expeditions. They and seventeen of their four-legged work companions arrived shortly thereafter, and Brad started his amusing interpretative talk on dogs, wolves and what he called the 'ugly' non-canine species called humans.

When it was time to start the dog sledding, Brad broke us into four groups of four people each. We went through an orientation which can be summed up in two points: One, put on as many clothes as possible (got that one aced), and two, keep your hands in the sleigh so you don't lose any digits when you go whipping down the trail. It sounded simple enough.

Brad then paired us up based upon body height and weight. There were only myself and two other women going dog sledding, so we seemed to be in demand as light ballast. I was matched up with Tyler, a tall lanky student who seemed rather shy. I soon discovered you can't stay shy when you're dog sledding with someone!

At the trailhead, we were put to work unloading sleds, harnessing dogs and shoveling doggie doo doo. They never mention that part in the brochures. Boy, can those skinny little dogs put out a lot of poop! Brad said it was because the dogs were nervous and were getting ready to run. It kept us running as we took turns shoveling, and doing the tasks assigned to us. Dog sledding is a lot like flying. Lots of prep time, not so much time actually doing what you came to do.

I got the heavy responsibility of trekking down the trail and posting a sign that says "Dogsledders on trail", a bit like putting out the red flag when diving. Not having done this before, I spent a few minutes pondering which bush or hill would be the best for visibility. Then I decided the number of moose likely to read the sign is rather small, so I stuck it in the nearest snow bank and headed back. By this time we were all getting rather cold and we hadn't even started yet. Someone started to hum "I'm a Popsicle, you're a Popsicle."

Preparations complete, Brad double checked that the sleds were anchored to the truck. Without that anchor, the dogs would take off as soon as he hooked them up even without us. That, Martha Stewart would say, "is a bad thing". Brad put the neck wires on the lead dogs and the whole pack went wild! I imagined it was a bit like being in the locker room before the Super Bowl; everyone was pumped and ready to run (the dogs) or ride (the humans).

Brad had us get into our sleds. Ha! It was a bit like getting on a toboggan, and then being zipped into a banana skin. If you don't know your sled partner when you start, you will by the time you are finished. We were wrapped around each other like a couple of pretzels trying to get comfortable. Tyler sat at the back of the sled for the journey out; I got the front seat, and the sleeping bag. Double bonus!

Finally we were ready, Brad picked up the snow anchor, and we were off. I barely had time to shoot one photo before we were up and over the first hill and knocked back in our seats. I tried not to squish Tyler, but after about the twentieth bump, I gave up and decided it was everyone for themselves.

With their high energy reserves, the dogs started eagerly, and raced down the trail like the wind…well, maybe a brisk breeze. There were three of us on the sled after all, and that slowed them down a bit. It was quiet except for the sound of the dogs panting, and the sun shining down on the fresh snow, making me feel like I was in the midst of a Christmas card. We travelled up and down over the hills and started to develop a rhythm.

We learned that black spruce trees on the side of the trail meant really wicked bumps. We learned how to lean into the turns, how to avoid trees, and how to wiggle your toes to keep the feeling in them.

After a bit, I realized that, while I was in constant contact with my tailbone, I had not felt my feet for sometime. I hoped that I wouldn't fall on my face when I got out of the sled.

Suddenly, we saw Susan's team coming our way. It's a real rush meeting another team on a trail that's only about two metres wide. One dog growled, Brad and Susan yelled commands to prevent head-on collisions, and then we were blasting off in opposite directions. I was impressed by how well the dogs worked and responded to commands.

We made the halfway mark all too quickly and turned for home. Brad stopped the team and then offered to let me help drive! Driving a dog team is a lot more active than driving a car. There is no steering wheel. The dogs respond to verbal commands, assuming you and they can remember them. I couldn't, so I focused on helping to 'pedal,' pushing with one leg to help the team.

The feeling came back to my toes quickly; they hurt like crazy. But it was a total thrill, whipping along the trail with my new furry friends running their hearts out. Brad told me the dogs can run for hours at a time without wearing out. Not me. After about five minutes of pedaling, I was breathing hard and using muscles I never knew I had. I asked Brad what he does to stay in shape for dog sledding. In hindsight it wasn't my brightest question. Brad told me that he dog sleds in order to stay in shape for dog sledding. That activity, and looking after a large kennel of almost one hundred dogs, doesn't leave much time or need for a fitness program.

Brad could tell by the fact that I was panting like the dogs that it was time for a new driver, so Tyler got his chance to mush. I took my place in the back of the sled so Brad could give verbal commands to the dogs, and throw out the anchor in the event of a wreck. The back seat was warmer with another person nestled in front, although the view was not as good. We spent the rest of the trip talking about past winter trips and dog lore. The time flew by. All too soon we were back at the trailhead; this was an experience everyone should have.

Trying On Other People's Lives

"Half the fun of the travel is the esthetic of lostness." ~ Ray Bradbury

Horse riding seems to be a common theme to many of my travel experiences. It is a fun way to spend an afternoon and it gives you a glimpse into another world. Horse breeds are different from country to country, and the way people train and ride their horses varies among cultures.

On one of my trips to northern Iceland I was working with tourism businesses to improve their products and marketing strategies and was offered the chance to ride one of the famous Icelandic ponies. I'd met some of ponies one evening on a barn tour, and found them very social, hanging over the stable slats to sniff my hand and receive a pat. They are smaller than the quarter horses I was used to, but they have an extra gait, a smooth, extended trot that allowed them to cover the rugged Icelandic hills quickly.

As our bus pulled up to the small Icelandic farm that was hosting our ride, I could see the horses gathered in a corral near the barn. This herd didn't seem to have the same friendly disposition I had seen in my earlier meeting with them. They were high spirited, and were running circles around the corral, trying to avoid capture by the farmer and his assistants.

We filed off the bus towards the paddock to gather our riding equipment, and wait for our horses. There didn't seem to be a quiet one in the bunch. None of them were inclined to come forward to have a halter put on. In fact, they did their best to run away. The fastest captures seemed to occur when one of the ranch hands would pretend to look away and then grab a horse as it came by, thinking it wasn't the target.

One of the handlers grabbed a particularly wild mount and bit its ear to quiet it, while quickly tossing a bridle on it. I was impressed. I had only ever seen that done in old John Wayne movies, and was amazed that it really worked.

When we were all matched up with a horse, saddling began. When I asked the farmer if my horse would stop when I called 'whoa', he scoffed and asked, "What kind of horse does that?"

"A trained one," I suggested. We obviously didn't share the same viewpoints on horse training, but I was beginning to wonder if the horses were the source of the Icelandic thirst for strong liquors. It appeared that even a short ride on an Icelandic pony will have you rediscovering religion and whisky, not necessarily in that order.

We mounted our little horses within the confines of the small paddock. Pulling on the reins seemed to only make the horses move faster and the fence seemed to be the only thing holding us back while our guides got their horses ready. I had discovered that pulling my horse in a tight circle seemed to be the only way to maintain anything that remotely resembled control.

A husky Norwegian I had met earlier went speeding by on his diminutive mount as they got to know each other. Within seconds the Norwegian was flying over the horse's head and rolling onto the ground. He picked himself up with a laugh and got back on again. A fellow Canadian, Colleen, looked at me and raised her eyebrows. I think we were both wondering what we had gotten ourselves into.

The gate was opened and there was a mad rush for the hills. The pace was fast, and the terrain rocky. A Quarter Horse would have broken a leg running up and down the treacherous terrain, but the Icelandic horses never missed a step. They tossed their heads and pulled at the reins, eager to outrace each other. I was not sure if the guide stayed at the front of the pack because of his skill, or if he just had the wildest horse.

The scenery was breathtaking although I did not have much time for sightseeing. I was spending much of my time holding my breath and struggling to keep my horse from running even faster. I discovered that if I steered his nose directly into the tail of the horse in front of me, he would slow down slightly. I could then pretend for a few seconds I was on a quiet trail ride, and look at the landscape around me.

After thirty minutes of continuous running up and down hills, our leader called a halt. It was the only time I saw the horses stop. Us getting off seemed to signal a rest break and they happily munched away on the green grass. I walked over to Colleen on legs that were shaking slightly, and asked how she was enjoyed the ride. "Joseph, Mary and Jesus," she said, "I've never seen anything like it!"

All too soon we were back in the saddle and headed for home. As I was getting used to the pell-mell pace across the barren grasslands, the horses saw the farm buildings, and picked up speed; something I had not thought possible. Any horse heading for the barn will often race. Having seen the normal velocity of the Icelandic ponies, I wasn't eager to experience their race speed.

I spotted one slower Icelandic horse ahead of me and headed for its tail, but my horse decided he was not going to dawdle when a meal was in the offing. He pulled around the slower horse and started to run in earnest.

I had been taught to slow a runaway horse by turning it in a circle. Even though this horse was small, it was strong. All I succeeded in doing was turning the horse's head sideways. We were now racing towards the fence with the horse running almost blind. I decided that was more dangerous than letting it run flat out, so I relaxed the reins and hung on. I was happy to see the barn was coming into focus, meaning the uncontrolled sprint was almost over.

All around me were horses and riders engaged in the same mad dash for the barns. Falling off now would mean a sure trampling. I could hear the voice of my riding instructor in my ear, "With all the training I've given you, you can ride any speed." I was hoping she was right.

I pushed my bottom more firmly into the saddle, and held on as we swung into the paddock. I quickly dismounted and walked over to Colleen who was leaning against her horse, trying to get her breath back.

"Let's go find ourselves some whiskey or schnapps," she said, "After that, I need something strong to settle my nerves!" I could not have agreed more, and we headed into the farmhouse kitchen to trade stories and celebrate our safe return.

My Red Sunglasses

"The scientific theory I like best is that the rings of Saturn are composed entirely of lost airline luggage." ~ Mark Russell

Experiencing the local culture is different when one doesn't speak the language. Communications may be limited to superficial exchanges of sign language, pantomime and foreign language dictionaries, but I've found inability to speak directly to people does not mean a person cannot have a satisfying travel experience. In fact, some of my best travel memories have come when I have found ways around language barriers.

English is common in most tourist destinations, so finding yourself in a place where no one speaks even a few words is a novel experience, a dramatic disconnection from our normal ways of relating to people and situations. I experienced this on a recent trip to Beijing.

"I'll have the cheese sandwich," I pantomimed, pointing at one of the two safest items on the menu. It was obvious my waitress spoke as much English as I spoke Mandarin – nada! I was not that hungry, but I was exhausted from the long trip to Beijing, and I wanted to eat before I ordered the stiff drink that was my reward for surviving the day's adventures. Nothing had gone as planned on this trip, and I was wondering if coming this far for a conference was a mistake.

No one from the conference organizers had met my flight as promised. Fortunately, I had the foresight to print off my hotel name and directions in Mandarin so I could take a taxi. No simple feat, it turned out. The crush of people pushing towards the taxi stand was overwhelming; but there seemed to be a sense of order, so I joined the long queue and patiently waited my turn.

The taxi driver took my English instructions and began looking at them with a very furrowed brow. I pointed to the Mandarin instructions on the bottom of the page. He looked at the page carefully, nodded what I took to be assent, and we headed out. I wasn't worried. Earlier, an official-looking person had given me directions and comfort when he said, "The taxis are metered, and the drivers will not try to cheat you."

The hotel website had said it was a 40 minute drive from the airport, but we weren't driving, we were sitting in heavy traffic, wondering if we would ever find the hotel. The sky had been grey when we landed mid afternoon. The pilot called it fog, but it looked and felt like soupy smog.

As the sun set, the city took on the feel of a medieval Oliver Twist town. The streets were dark and people on bikes and on foot would come into sight for a few seconds before being swallowed up again by the night. Wisps of fog seemed to wrap around the few street lights, giving them a ghostly appearance. The drivers on the freeway seemed to be engaged in some sort of choreographed traffic dance, sharing lanes at times, and merging at high speeds, but never coming close enough to crash.

As I went to reread my instructions, I realized with great dismay that I had left my reading glasses on the airplane. This was going to be a problem since my arms had shrunk to the point where I could not read normal print without glasses. My driver finally found the hotel and I almost went into cardiac arrest when I tried to read the meter. It looked like I owed him $1,000!

Desperate for rest. I started out counting all the Yuan I had. The driver, an honest sort, stopped me after I'd given him 200 Yuan or about $25. I was relieved to see I would be able to afford food now. Obviously I didn't have a clue how to read a Chinese taxi meter.

I checked into the sumptuous Loong Palace Hotel and Resort, complete with indoor pool, bowling alley, tennis courts, theatre and karaoke bar. I hit the gift shops hoping to find a pair of reading glasses. Best I could find was a magnifying glass, but I didn't want to look like Sherlock Holmes reading my speech.

I went over to the porter to enlist his help in getting to the nearby mall. "Is there someplace I can get glasses?" I asked.

"Yes there is," he said. "I can write the name of the mall in Mandarin and ask the taxi driver to wait for you while you shop." This seemed like a workable plan. The porter flagged a taxi, explained my situation and I hopped in, clutching my mandarin addresses tightly in my hand. I felt like one of those small kids who go to school with their home address pinned to their shirt, but I figured if it works, who cares?

This driver wasted no time in getting from point A to B. We skirted around major roads in favor of small winding streets. I had one of those anxious moments when I thought "If something happened to me out here, my family won't even know where to start searching for me." I decided to take a more optimistic outlook, and enjoy the sights.

The mall turned out to be a very modern building, but parking was a problem. There was much honking and jockeying for rare curb space. My driver seemed to be double parked in the melee and I asked if I should get out here and run into the store. My driver responded with a long tirade of Mandarin and much waving of hands. "I'll take that as a no," I thought, and settled back to see what would happen next.

Our path forward was blocked, but we were able to reverse so we maneuvered our way to the parkade entrance backward. We drove onto an underground ramp that circled the building and soon popped up on the other side where parking was more abundant. When the taxi stopped, I made a walking motion with my fingers trying to say I would hurry into the store and come right back. I had not paid him so I was pretty sure he would wait.

I scurried into the mall and my extensive shopping skills paid off. Even without bring able to read any of the signs, I made a beeline for the drugstore and stopped a clerk. By putting my fingers in circles around my eyes like a raccoon, I indicated I was looking for glasses. The clerk nattered on in Mandarin. I understood nothing of it, but assumed she was telling me I was out of luck.

I scored gold two doors down, a glasses store! I almost wept with relief when I scanned the cases and saw reading glasses. They were three power with rather ugly, heavy brown frames. They looked like something an old man with stooped shoulders, loafers and a ratty cardigan would wear, but beggars can't be choosers. The eager salesclerk who had materialized at my side was pulling out glasses. I held up two fingers and pointed at the magnification. She actually understood and found a more feminine looking pair with a flowery pattern along the arm. These would do the trick.

At the till as I opened my wallet to pay, the clerk pulled out a box with a pair of cherry red sunglasses with rhinestones at the corners. With their cat-shaped lenses, they would look great on some wild-at-heart librarian if she got a spin in a sporty convertible. I was not planning on adding them to my wardrobe, but the clerk said 'sunglasses' the only English I had heard all evening; and put them in with my purchase.

I looked up to see my taxi driver waiting at the store entrance. I was not sure if I was taking too long, or if he was worried at what had become of me; but we smiled at each other and he escorted me back to the taxi.

I was not nervous anymore. I realized I had learned enough to get by in Beijing, and that the people were some of the friendliest I had ever met. I pulled out my new, red sunglasses and smiled at the knowledge my girlfriends were going to die laughing when I wear them to our next coffee date.

Section Four - Realization

"When you look like your passport photo, it's time to go home." ~ *Erma Bombeck*

Mom's Always Right, *page 130*

People travel for many reasons. Business travellers may have little control over when or where they go, but the person travelling for leisure is a complex creature. We hit the roads to see our friends and family, have fun, learn new things, discover new places, or meet new people.

Do we undertake trips with the idea of changing ourselves or the world? We may be just looking to change our circumstances. If we're stressed from our jobs or personal responsibilities, we may choose a package holiday where all the major decisions have already been made, and we can focus on sleep, sunbathing and eating.

When we're bored with our everyday life, travel can be a way to raise the excitement level. We look for a trip that will teach us something, or provide an adventure, physical or emotional; or we may look for a tour that has like-minded people who might be potential friends or romantic interests.

I have probably taken a trip at one time or another for all of those reasons. I have found that from the second you leave home for a trip, travel does change you. Sometimes the change is so small you may not realize it started from something you did or saw on your holiday. You enjoyed eating fresh seafood everyday at an ocean-side resort, and when you get home, you start eating more fish.

Other times, the changes are unmistakable. I was not born a bird watcher. On my earliest trips to Africa, I was bored silly while everyone around me oohed and aahed over the sighting of a 'lifer', a species that they had not seen before. I leaned more to the philosophy of my travelling companion, Jane, who referred to Nightjars as the Oil of Olay bird! It would be several more trips before I developed an appreciation for birds, and now, my binoculars are one of the first things I pack for every trip. I am not a serious 'twitcher', but I have a new hobby that definitely arose from my travels. And I have developed a pretty decent life list.

Sometimes the changes that arise from travel are internal, and may not be visible to other people. Often, the first time people from the developed world travel to poverty-stricken regions, they are shocked at the living conditions. Many people come home with a new appreciation for their own living conditions. Some adopt a more environmentally and socially-conscious approach to life. They may buy fewer consumer goods or become more active in humanitarian work. Some start travelling in a new fashion, volunteering while on holiday to help other communities or ecology projects.

I have also seen the effects of travel first-hand on the communities I have worked with as a tourism consultant. For rural communities near natural areas, tourists can be very important sources of economic activity. The income from a few travellers seeking adventure or culture can create jobs that can keep young people in the community, or mitigate the problems caused when traditional industries disappear.

While people will always travel for escape or discovery, there is a growing awareness that travel choices can also be used for change, both within and in the global context. I think the next travel frontier will be travel that helps people explore their relationships and the deeper meaning of their lives.

Defining Moments

"All journeys have secret destinations of which the traveler is unaware."
~ Martin Buber

Renowned photographer Henri Cartier-Bresson said that the only photos worth taking are those that capture defining moments. A person could look at something like Niagara Falls, a tourism attraction of great beauty that has been photographed millions of times by tourists; but for Cartier-Bresson, it would be only be interesting to photograph it if there was something definitive, say somebody going over in a barrel. To him, that would define the relationship between people and the environment in an unusual way.

Many of us will find our travels provide defining moments for our lives; things are not the same for us after the trip as they were before. We are changed in some fundamental way. For Kevin Crockett, Director of Product and Destination Development for Alberta Tourism, Parks, Recreation and Culture Department, one of his defining moments occurred early in his career.

Meeting Kevin, you quickly learn that he loves to travel. He says one of his proudest moments was when he took his daughter, Brittany to Rome, a city that Kevin and his wife love for its rich history and culture. "She totally got it," Kevin explained. "She found the ruins and the architecture and the human history of the area as interesting as we do. I was so proud of her."

But unlike his daughter, Kevin was not introduced to international travel at a young age. Soon after Kevin completed his undergraduate degree in geography, he started work for the Alberta government as a park planner. One day he got a call one day from Lorna, a young woman who was researching rock glaciers and was interested in a university paper he had published on the subject. Moreover, she wanted Kevin to accompany her on a field trip to study a nearby rock glacier in the front range of Alberta's mountains.

Kevin spent three days in the mountains with Lorna; and, while the time passed amicably enough, he decided he was not that enthralled with this particular woman. As it turned out, Lorna had a similar reaction. They parted ways at the end of the study, and Kevin continued at the Parks department planning future developments and conservation strategies.

A few weeks later, Lorna dropped by the office unannounced. This time something clicked and five months later they were married. When they got home from their honeymoon trip to Victoria, British Columbia, a letter was waiting for them. "I had entered a draw," Kevin said, "for a holiday to Hong Kong. There it was; notification that we'd won!"

Plans were quickly made. That was 1983 and few westerners had travelled on their own to China.

"We were delighted to find a culture that was so distinct and different from our own," Kevin said, "In some of the places we visited, I think we were the first white travellers people had seen." This total immersion in the culture created a brief sense of disorientation followed by a feeling of elation.

"We were both interested in these limestone 'forests' in the Kumnimg area so we would take a bus out to hike in the area. We would memorize the route the bus driver took so that we could walk back to our starting point," Kevin said. "It was a fantastic trip."

Many people who have visited China would agree it is a beautiful experience, but for Kevin it was more than that. The trip sparked an interest in foreign cultures and travel that he had not felt before. Despite being someone who spent his professional life creating better places for travellers, Kevin had not fully appreciated the excitement of travel until this point. He had enjoyed travel; but now he had passion for exploring the world and its far-flung attractions.

When Lorna and Kevin got back from China they knew they wanted to make this type of travel a priority. Each year they explore new and different destinations. They have been kayaking in eastern Canada, toured Australia, Europe and Asia, hiked to Machu Picchu and scuba dived in the South Pacific.

The birth of their daughter Brittany did not slow down their world travel. "I remember one day in Tonga when Lorna and I were diving. I came up to the water's surface and there was four year old Brittany swimming around the boat with a lifejacket and water wings under the watchful eye of the ship's captain," Kevin said. This exposure to travel would pay off, as Brittany has developed the same love of travel that was sparked in her parents many years earlier in China.

The Ends Of The Earth

"The traveller was active; he went strenuously in search of people, of adventure, of experience. The tourist is passive; he expects interesting things to happen to him. He goes 'sight-seeing'." ~ Daniel J. Boorstin

Keith Dewing is a geologist and a professional traveller. Since 1986, he has been spending summers as a research scientist in Canada's high Arctic. His form of travel is more rugged than most; there are no Starbucks or swimming pools, not even guaranteed flight departures. The northern beauty and isolation have made for a memorable career, and the opportunity to learn much about human nature.

"Travel to the Arctic in the 1980s wasn't much different than travel to the region in the 1880s," he says. "Scientists put up with harsh weather, insects, travel on rough terrain, and crowded living conditions."

Keith explains, "Usually a research team will establish a base camp with a number of large double-sided 14 by 16 foot canvas tents. Two tents will be linked together to create a large room for eating and working in the evenings. Another tent will become the shower tent. A large diesel generator will be moved in to heat water and provide warmth for the all too brief showers. A wooden pallet becomes the shower floor."

Life in camp takes on a predictable rhythm. Keith is up before seven a.m. to make the daily call letting head office know that everyone is doing well. Then a quick breakfast, and packing the bags for the day's work. Helicopters start taking people out to field sites around nine. After a full day of taking samples and mapping landforms people return to camp around six.

Dinners are hearty and unexpected treats like Cherries Jubilee for dessert contrasts to the ruggedness. It's an unwritten rule that the cook never does dishes, so everyone pitches in on camp chores before spending some time looking at the day's data and planning the next days work. If time and energy permit, a couple of card games offer some relaxation, before everyone turns in for the night.

"It can be difficult to keep a routine up north," Keith says. "With the long hours of daylight, some people start working later and later, because the conditions can be better at night, but I find it is better to try and stay on a normal work schedule. It is tiring work and if you are going to be working for two months straight, it's important to conserve your energy."

Bugs can be an unpleasant part of northern travel. High Arctic islands are often too cold and windy for mosquitoes and biting flies, but islands in lower latitudes can have bugs at legendary levels. On one trip to Southampton Island, Keith had one of his most memorable mosquito encounters. "They were so numerous; it was almost like someone was standing behind you. When you woke up in the morning it sounded like it was raining, but it was the mosquitoes hitting the tent, trying to get in."

Mosquito repellent does not slow down these northern pests, and screened hats and clothing are hot. Keith goes without repellent, and makes it a practice not to scratch the bites. "Once you start, you can't stop," he says.

Keith also uses a unique sampling tool to decide if the bugs are too bad to work outside. "We would take one of our geological survey books, stick it quickly outside the tent and snap it shut. Then we'd bring it inside and count how many dead insects we caught on the eight by eight inch surface. My record was 40 but one fellow claimed to have caught 160 on a trip to Labrador one year!" If there were too many mosquitoes caught in the book, they would look for work they could do inside.

Sometimes scientists go on trips with very limited equipment, and give up the amenities of base camp. "We call this fly camping. A helicopter will drop off a few people with small tents and their gear to gather data. The tents we use for this are called 'Logans,' named after the founder of the Geological Survey. They are built so they can't be blown down, no matter how high the winds get," Keith says. And the Arctic has some extremely high winds.

The Logans would not win any prizes in a most-appealing tent contest. They have one center pole and the walls are different lengths, giving it an asymmetrical look. The long sloping back is placed toward the prevailing winds to deflect them. The wide doorway on the short stubby side is big enough to give you a clear view of or shot at any dangerous wildlife approaching downwind.

When a crew lands, someone takes a wind reading to determine in which direction to set up the tents. In the north, the winds are often from the west.

"This is the value of experience," Keith says, "The new people put their Logan with the back towards the west. But most storms come from the opposite direction, so the high winds come ripping into the door of the tent, inflating it, and making it noisy and a really uncomfortable place to stay. You see these people running around trying to put 45 gallon fuel drums on their tent to keep them from flying away because once the storm starts you can't move the tents." It goes to show that having the right type of tent and pitching your tent in the right spot is critical for enjoying your time in the North.

Keith remembers one trip where he went fly camping on Cornwallis Island at 75 degrees north latitude, well within the Arctic Circle. For shelter, he and another geologist had only a pup tent; a larger tent was used for a working and cooking space. "The night we were dropped off was so nice we ate outside, and didn't bother to set up the larger tent before we went to bed. During the night, a huge storm came up and the winds were terrible. The instruments on the plane parked nearby showed 100 km/hour winds. We spent the next two days lying in our sleeping bags, unable to do anything because of the wind. It was pretty unpleasant to spend all that time laying on your back, with the tent canvas pushed by the wind to only a few inches from our faces, but we couldn't set up the large tent in that weather. We learned not to leave the tent pitching for the second day!" Keith said.

Although people might think wild animals are a big threat for Arctic travel, that is not the case. "I worked in the north five years before I saw a bear," Keith says, "I was working with another geologist on Cornwallis Island taking measurements. The fellow was reading off data in a regular voice tone and in the same casual voice he says 'Bear'. What?" I asked. I looked up from my notes to see a large polar bear running towards us.

We had left our rifles in the ATVs a few hundred metres away, so we started to run as fast as we could back towards the vehicles. Those bears can really move. We were running towards the ATVs, and so was the bear, so really we were running towards the bear while it was running towards us."

"We made it there first, and our adrenaline was running high. We thought instead of getting out the gun, it would be best to start the ATVs and outrun the bear. I grabbed the throttle and fired up my ATV, but the other fellow wasn't able to get his going. He was swearing and desperately trying to fire up the machine. I reached over and flipped his kill switch. His machine started and we were off. As soon as the bear heard the engines start it turned and ran off. I found out later that because many of the bears have been tranquilized at one time or another by scientists, they associate machinery with bad bear experiences!"

"We made it back to camp where we told some of the other people about our encounter," Kevin said. "An older man asked if we had been scared when we saw the bear. I said I had been, but my work partner had calmed down a lot from when he was frantically trying to start his ATV, and now said seeing the bear had been no big deal."

"The old man said, 'If you say you're not scared of a bear, you're lying!' He said you can't be that close to a big bear and not feel some fear. I think he's right."

For many people the real challenge of northern travel is the isolation and the lack of control over events. "I was working at a camp near the Armed Forces base at Alert and we would get these weird solar storms and visual effects like inversions, which sometimes meant you saw things in the air that weren't really there," Keith said. "Once there was an inversion and we could see the clouds lit up over the base. It actually looked like a mushroom cloud in the air above the base. Later that day we lost radio contact."

"Seeing a mushroom cloud over an army base and then losing radio contact could have been a coincidence, or perhaps, it could have been something more significant. We thought maybe it was the result of a solar storm which would interfere with radio contact from time to time; but we actually wondered if the outside world was still there," Keith said.

"We were without radio contact for two whole weeks, so eventually we decided to fly over to another camp and see if they were still there, and to see what they had heard," he said. "They were happy to see us. While they hadn't seen the oddly-shaped cloud, they too had been without radio contact for many days. We had a cook at our camp so we had brought them freshly-baked dessert and made them very happy. We flew back to our camp, and eventually the radios came back to life."

Not knowing what is happening or not being able to control events puts many people off northern travel. Help is quickly available for most emergencies when conditions are good, but when bad weather knocks out the radios or makes it unsafe to fly, northern travellers are isolated.

"When a storm hits, you know you're on your own until it's over," Keith says. This can be hard for many people to deal with, along with the difficulty in making firm travel plans.

"When it is time to go home, the camp is packed up, and everyone waits for the plane to pick them up. But the wait can be a long one," Keith explains. "The geologists are the last priority. If there is a medical emergency or supplies to be dropped off, the plane goes there first. If the pilot has flown his allowable hours for the day, the plane gets parked. Sometimes we will wait all day only to have to unpack everything, and set up camp for another night. In the morning the whole process is repeated. I've learned to live with it. One trip I waited for seven days to be picked up, unpacking each morning, waiting all day, and remaking camp each evening when it became apparent we weren't going to be picked up."

In the north, the illusion that we control of our world is stripped away, and people are left to fend for, and to face themselves.

"The hard times force you to think about what you really like. I've learned to be more patient and forgiving from my Arctic travel. An expression I often use to get me through the tough times is 'I've always seen worse!'"

"Two months in an isolated place is a lot of time to think about what you want to do," Keith concludes. "I've also never found someone who changed from the travel. I think it just makes you more honest about yourself."

Lessons Learned On The River

"It always rains on tents. Rainstorms will travel thousands of miles, against prevailing winds for the opportunity to rain on a tent." ~ Dave Barry

To me, the business behind travel is as interesting as the travel itself, and I love to teach a class in Adventure Travel each summer at the University of Calgary. We spend one concentrated week learning about risk management, resource planning, tourism issues, and the nature of adventure. To give everyone a shared adventure, we spend a day out of the classroom, taking part in an outdoor activity like whitewater rafting. Everyone has a chance to think about what constitutes an adventure.

One year, we headed out for a two-hour whitewater rafting trip. Heavy rain had swollen the river, but our tour operator said it was still safe to go paddling. "The ride might be a little faster than usual, but it's still safe."

I had stayed at the base camp to mark exams and suddenly I realized the camp radio was unusually busy, with lots of rapid fire communications coming in.

"What's happening?" I asked a guide. "A raft flipped over," he said, "But it's okay. They've picked up everybody, but one person."

I don't know how he defined okay, but if there were upside-down rafts in a river, it is not okay until everyone is accounted for! Perhaps he was afraid I might come over the desk at him if he did not act calm, but his answer did not make me feel better. Most of the rafters on the river that morning were my students, and I knew there was a good chance the flipped raft had been from my group.

As I fretted and paced for what seemed like hours, probably only a few minutes, trying to get my head around things. I could not believe a raft had flipped. I was horrified to think that students entrusted to me might be injured or worse, and I didn't even want to contemplate the paperwork and legal repercussions.

Finally, the radio crackled to life. "We've got everybody" someone reported.

I felt like doing a jig, but settled down to wait for the shuttle bus. Everyone was being brought back to camp right away to warm up, and for a debriefing. I asked "Was the flipped raft carrying my students?" "Yes," was the brief reply.

When the bus pulled up, wet and cold rafters tumbled out. Some of their faces looked pinched and their eyes wide; others looked remarkably unconcerned. The head of the rafting company gathered everyone around the fire to talk about the trip. From the bits of conversation that everyone was sharing, I gathered that the second boat in the group had run into a sweeper, a tree that had fallen down across the river.

The guide was knocked out of the boat first and then everyone else went in. The lead boat was able to pick up some people almost immediately. Other rafters swam to shore or climbed on rocks or trees until someone could rescue them. There were a few bumps and bruises, but physically people seemed to be okay. The emotional effects were much greater.

People who were experienced rafters seemed to be the most shaken. They described their panic at finding themselves in the water. "I knew we were supposed to float downstream with our legs in front of us and yet I found myself trying to swim upstream," one person said. "I couldn't get out of the current; it was too strong," another added. It seemed they knew how much trouble they were in.

The students who were new to rafting seemed to be more philosophical in many ways. They were counting on the guides to handle any problems, and when the rescue unfolded as planned, their stress level came down quickly. Their trip diaries had lots of extra details on where they were during the flip and subsequent rescue, and many said they would try the river again. They seemed more confident than I had expected. It was as if they had survived their worst fear, so they were keen to try again.

Unexpectedly, some of the most profound effects of our river adventure were on students who didn't end up in the river. Many said "We felt helpless watching the boat hitting the tree and then flipping." They realized how random misfortune can be.

Others students felt empowered by the experience. A couple of students in the lead boat had jumped into action when the boat flipped, helping the guide pull people out of the water, and then bushwhacking back upstream to make sure everyone was accounted for.

One fellow felt profound satisfaction at having his outdoor skills put to the test. He was an active paddler and had practiced rescue drills, but this was the first time people's lives depended upon his actions. He wrote "I want to thank you for this experience. This class has proved to be one of adventure. Your method of teaching is spectacular which I only could have wished would have come sooner."

It wasn't the trip I had planned for this class, but we all learned more than I could have imagined about adventure on the river that day.

The Bear Facts

"Like all great travelers, I have seen more than I remember, and remember more than I have seen." ~ Benjamin Disraeli

Bill Bryan, founder of Off The Beaten Path adventure tour company, had an unexpected lesson while leading a trip from Camp Denali in the Alaska wilderness.

Located in the heart of Denali National Park in Alaska, Camp Denali is a remarkable facility with an interesting history. Its seventeen cabins and a central lodge offer travellers the chance to experience Alaskan wilderness in comfort with rustic ambience. Decorated with Alaskan artwork, each cabin comes with its own outhouse, and view of Mt. McKinley, weather permitting. It is one of only two lodges in the park to have such vistas. A bus picks up visitors at Denali Park Rail station, and drives the almost-seven hours to the camp for great opportunities to see wildlife and to get a sense of the wilderness.

Most suppliers to Camp Denali are at least nine hours distant, so the staff has to be self-sufficient and works hard to keep visitors happy. As a result, guests are treated to incredible hospitality and some of the U.S.'s best outdoor experiences.

Camp Denali was established in 1951 by the legendary Ginny Wood, Celia Hunter and Morton Wood. Ginny Wood was a WASP pilot in World War II, and after the war she, along with her friends, travelled through Europe. Their admiration for the hut system they encountered there, inspired them to create Camp Denali.

The camp was one of the first North American lodges to adopt ecotourism principles, and their adherence to strict environmental standards has resulted in a great working relationship with the Park managers. It is the only Lodge allowed to dock canoes at Wonder Lake or take guests hiking in the area behind the Wonder Lake arm of the Park road. Camp Denali is the Park's sole historic operator of guided hiking and educational trips. Bill takes his guests to Camp Denali because of its guiding privileges, and it is here that he had one of his most memorable travel experiences.

Bill was enjoying a day hike with twelve clients. They had climbed almost 250 metres (about 800 feet) to a hilltop when a hoary marmot's sharp whistle told Bill's group they were regarded as a source of danger even though the group meant no harm with their binoculars and cameras.

A short while later they spotted a wolverine in the distance. Encountering this seldom-seen species was a first for many people and the mood was euphoric. The lodge guide had remarked that this was the first sighting of a wolverine this summer.

The group had loaded back onto the small bus for more touring when they came across a grizzly bear taking down a moose calf. The drama unfolded within a few metres of the bus giving everyone ringside seats in a bloody, life-and-death struggle.

The calf was screaming as the bear attacked it with its claws and teeth. The grizzly was covered in the moose's blood as it attempted to drag the moose into the bush.

"I was amazed at the reaction of my clients to the bear attack," Bill recalls. "Some people felt bad for the poor baby moose as it fought unsuccessfully for its life. One person commented how an African lion is much more efficient in its killing. But efficient is a human word. That grizzly was just being a bear. It got its prey in the best way it knew how. We as humans anthropomorphize, we evaluate." Bill later recalled, "I even remember thinking that I could kill that moose more cleanly."

Bill's group drove down the road a little further and spotted an adult moose with a bloody gash on its side.

"We figured it was the mother. The bear had probably surprised her and her calf, and she had got the wound attempting to defend her young against the attack. The next day when we passed again through the area the bear was laying by the side of the road, stretched out to his full length and looking fat and lazy. He appeared to be sleeping off his large meal," Bill said.

"Although the group was still saddened over the death of the moose calf," Bill said. "We realized that what we had seen was a unique opportunity to observe nature. We started to realize how lucky the bear had been to get a successful kill. My guests didn't like seeing the kill, but they understood it."

And perhaps that is one of the ways travel influences us. We don't always like the rawness we see but in seeing it, we gain a better appreciation for the world around us

Mom's Always Right

"When preparing to travel, lay out all your clothes and all your money. Then take half the clothes and twice the money." ~ Susan Heller

Remember how your mom always told you to be careful around sharp objects or you would poke your eye out? Usually these universal admonishments from parents to their kids were the fastest way to make us want to do something we are not supposed to. At least that's how I always reacted to my mom's well-intentioned advice when I was a kid.

I like to think I've outgrown that phase of my life, but travel situations can raise spectres of your past you thought were long since buried. I found this out the hard way on a trip to Australia in 1998.

My mom had always wanted to see the Land Down Under and when I lucked into some airline tickets from Canada to Australia, here was her chance.

My mom and I looked at the trip with excitement and dread. The long flight from North America to Sydney means you have to be a movie lover, or really good at sleeping in glorified lawn chairs. We arrived at the Sydney airport early in the morning feeling tired and jetlagged but the sun shone brightly, and the warm weather cheered us up. We splurged on a taxi to our hotel and tumbled into bed for a long nap followed by a long sleep.

We spent our first conscious day in Sydney riding a red double-decker bus, checking out the sights, and hoping off frequently for a bit of shopping. This was a new type of travel for my mom and I to do together and it took awhile to find a rhythm. We both had things we wanted to do and see, but we were trying hard to be considerate of the other person's wishes.

I think Mom was being more considerate of me, than vice versa. In my experience, it takes about two decades living on your own before you stop taking advantage of a parent's ingrained willingness to do anything for their children. This selfishness was brought to front and center of my consciousness by the most unexpected of messengers.

I convinced mom that the Taronga Zoo it would be a great start to our wildlife watching in Australia. Early the next day we caught the ferry at Circular Quay over to the zoo. We got to the zoo before the weather started heating up, our day's route planned.

The Taronga Zoo is laid out on a steep hillside with the exhibits built over several hundred feet elevation from top to bottom. It was steep walking, so it was clear that we wanted to maximize our time walking downhill and avoid backtracking or climbing as much as possible.

We located the Koala bears, our must-see animal; they looked so cute sleeping, we took about a dozen photos of their sweet faces from various angles, and then got ready for some action photos. We waited and we waited to see them do something. Anything. After a while, we realized that the rise and fall of their bellies with their breath, or the turning of their heads was as much action as we were going to see. Still we shot off another dozen frames to fill the time.

At lunch we headed for the cafeteria which had a nice indoor restaurant and some really charming outdoor areas; tables were nestled in amongst the trees shading the terrace.

I ordered a burger and fries and asked my mom where she wanted to sit.

"I think we should eat inside," she said, "I think there will be too many bugs and things outside."

This is probably where I should have said "What a great idea, mom! Why don't I go grab that corner table over there and wait for you?" Instead the rebellious kid inside of me said something more like, "Nonsense, there won't be any problem with the critters or bugs. It's Australia and it would be soooo nice to sit outside. I'll go get a table outside while you get your order." Which I promptly did.

I was putting the ketchup on my fries when my mom arrived and sat down at the table on the almost deserted patio. I did not recognize that emptiness for the foreboding that it was. Instead, I saw the beautiful blue sky, the leafy green trees and heard the call of birds nearby.

I was putting the third or forth French fry in my mouth when I felt like I had been hit in the face with a hockey stick. Stunned, it took me a moment to realize I had just been mugged by a Kookaburra bird. One had been sitting on the tree, innocently I thought, but obviously this guy made his living, snatching food out of people's hands or off their trays. This time he miscalculated slightly and hit me in the face instead of making a clean snatch and grab!

A Kookaburra can deliver a significant body blow. They are the size of a big chicken and have a long, sharp bill. Snatching French fries should have been pretty easy work; they're used to catching snakes in the bush. My mouth was throbbing, and I could feel blood coming out of the split in my lip.

People came rushing over see if I was all right, and offer me extra napkins to mop up the mess. I sheepishly said to Mom, "Perhaps we should eat inside. The bugs are not bad, but the birds are killer."

I figured that God was getting me for not listening to my mother; and I vowed to be a better travelling companion after that, lest He send sharks or freshwater crocodiles to teach me the next lesson!

My Mom told my Dad on the phone a few hours later about my run-in with the Kookaburra. My Dad called my husband Colin to report the incident.

Apparently the phone reception had not been great because by the time I reached Colin the next day, he wanted to know how I had come to be attacked by a koala bear!

After seeing the koalas "in action" I could not stop laughing; the risk from those 'bears" was small and nothing! The real terrors were sitting innocently in the trees; a threat disguised as scenery. Good thing there are mothers to tell you what is dangerous and what isn't.

Dancing In The Serengeti

"Certainly, travel is more than the seeing of sights; it is a change that goes on, deep and permanent, in the ideas of living." ~ Miriam Beard

In addition to learning from our elders, there are other lessons waiting for us on trips. Sometimes the information is easy to overlook, or we do not realize what we are seeing. This was the case for me when I discovered more about the working conditions of many tourism professionals in the developing world.

"Look at those wildebeest," Colin said, "As far as you can see there are animals, wildebeest, zebra, gazelle..."

His voice trailed off as he gazed spellbound at the migration that happens like clockwork each year in East Africa. Almost a million animals follow the rains and the resulting green grass through the Masai Mara, down into the Serengeti and back again, in a cycle that is as old as time.

Our Land Rover had broken down shortly after we reached the Serengeti in northern Tanzania. We were indulging ourselves in some extra wildlife viewing while our ever-capable drivers huddled under the hood trying to fix the problem. With no quick fix in sight, our trip leader, photographer Carol Petersen, suggested we eat our picnic lunches. Comfort food has a role, even on an African safari!

As we watched the drivers tinker with the engine, another Land Rover pulled up. It was taking workers from the Lodge we were staying at to the bus station for the start of their annual leave. There was much nattering back and forth in Swahili until finally one of the drivers came to tell Carol that it had been agreed that we would switch vehicles. Our group would take the working vehicle and continue our wildlife tour to the Lodge. The workers would wait for a mechanic to be sent out and they would then drive ours. We were eager to get to the Lodge for a cold drink and a swim, so we made the trade and set off.

A couple of hours later, we were comfortably ensconced in and around the pool admiring the landscaping and putting the finishing touches on our Serengeti synchronized swimming routine. Spirits were high as we chatted about what we had seen and what we might discover next in the legendary Serengeti.

You'd think we were rock stars, the way we were treated by the hotel staff with warmth and excitement. Carol seemed to be a very popular tour leader, judging by the wide smiles and the "jambo habari Ms Carol" that rang out frequently. Our Serengeti stay was shaping up to be something very special.

After we lowered our body temperatures with some pool time, Colin and I settled into a couple of pool chairs and pulled out our binoculars for some poolside birding. The pool attendant came by to take our order, and lingered to ask us where we came from.

"Canada," I replied, "Are you from around here?"

"No," he said, "I am from a village many hours drive from here."

I was curious to know more and asked "How long have you worked at the lodge? Do you have a family living here at the Lodge?" His reply startled me.

"I have worked at this Lodge for 16 years," he said, "I have a family, but due to the environmental regulations of the Park, staff housing is limited. Our families cannot live here so we are only able to see them on holidays."

In Canada, many people work away from home but usually get to visit with their family every week or two.

"How often do you get time off?" I asked.

"We get six weeks off once a year," he said, "Sometimes we might get a day off to visit the nearest village when we need to do a pick up or delivery. Some families move to these nearby villages so they can see their loved ones more often."

I was shocked. Almost eleven months between visits with your spouse and your children! It was almost beyond my comprehension how someone could live this way, year in and year out. As I thought about it, tourism jobs are very well paid; and, while the amount of time left for families is very small, the financial rewards of such a job would give the families a much better life.

I had a sudden pang of guilt when I thought about our switch of vehicles earlier. It had not appeared to be a big deal at the time; but for the workers who had to wait for the vehicle repairs, giving up hours of their much anticipated holiday, it must have been very disappointing and a huge sacrifice.

I realized then how small many of my hardships are. Yet there does not seem to be a correlation between perceived hardships and happiness. Our newfound friend didn't seem unhappy with his situation. In fact he was cheerful and more upbeat than many wealthy Canadians I have met.

Shortly after supper, Carol announced, "I have a surprise for you. Follow me to the pool." Eager to see what night-time adventures might be awaiting us, we hustled on down to the pool; but the sight stopped us in our tracks.

The patio around the pool had been transformed into an open-air disco. Tiny lights twinkled from the trees and toilet paper had been strung between branches in a rather unorthodox, but festive, touch; sort of like a Saturday Night Fever meets Halloween. A portable tape player was belting out some loud dance tunes, and a couple of muscular guys were unloading cases of beer and pop. The staff was starting to gather, many of them hitting the dance floor as soon as they crossed the disco 'entrance', hips swaying and feet moving to the beat.

"It's my thank you to them" Carol explained, "On the last night of every visit here, I sponsor this disco for the staff."

It was easy to see why all the staff had such warm greetings for Carol when we arrived. If I had worked 46 weeks between days off, a chance to blow off steam would be much appreciated. I would probably name my first born after the person kind enough to organize it.

Our tour group and the staff danced and danced, and danced some more. We joined the conga lines snaking through the crowd. We gamely danced with any person or group brave enough to ask us onto the dance floor. We laughed when our guides displayed their silly versions of animal dances, and we saw life on the Serengeti in a way not mentioned in any of the travel brochures.

The chance to party with these hard-working Africans under the Serengeti night sky with toilet paper decorations is something I'll never forget. And whenever I am tempted to complain about my problems, I think of the pool-side attendant.

Changing Through Fish Tourism

"If we are always arriving and departing, it is also true that we are eternally anchored. One's destination is never a place but rather a new way of looking at things." ~ *Henry Miller*

Jan Negrijn, founder of Coastal Connections, an ecotourism company in Newfoundland & Labrador, is a big believer in travel's ability to change people and entire communities. The transplanted Englishman grew up near the sea, became a commercial fisherman in Washington State and then pursued a career in marine sciences, working as an instructor at the Marine Institute at Memorial University in St. John's, Newfoundland & Labrador.

At the Institute, he would regularly take school groups on tours and show them the wonders of the ocean.

"Some of these kids are too cool for their own clothes," Jan says. "Yet once they've been shown some of the small invertebrates from the sea up close, they get so excited." After years of doing tours through the Marine Institute, Jan wanted to do more of these trips and under his own terms.

He bought his own boat, the MV Coastal Explorer, and established Coastal Connections. Jan chose not to focus on whale watching like other tour companies. Instead, Coastal Connections starts with the small creatures and teaches people how the smallest and largest creatures are related in the web of life. Looking at plankton may not seem like an exciting way to spend a trip, but Jan is able to turn the time on the water into fun for everyone.

"This is better than the Discovery Channel," one woman said; and, judging from the awards Coastal Connection has won for excellence in tourism, many people agree.

Jan says some of his most satisfying moments have come not on the sea, but on land, in the small village of Petley where Coastal Adventures is based. The town is located on Random Island on the east coast of Newfoundland, about two hours drive from the province's capital, St. John's.

Like many rural outports, Petley was hard hit by the cod fishing moratorium of the 1990s. For generations, Petley residents had made a living fishing for northern cod in the waters of Smith Sound. Protected by spruce-clad hills, the sound produced abundant cod and people made a living and raised their families in the small community.

When the cod disappeared in the 1990s, many young families left to find work elsewhere. Those who remained blamed the government for mismanaging the fish stocks and distrusted scientists for failing to protect the fishermen's livelihood.

As a scientist, Jan was prepared for some cynicism from the Petley residents so he took the time to explain to people what he was trying to accomplish with his company. For people who had spent their lives eking out a living on the open water often in miserable conditions, it was hard for them to believe people would pay good money for tours of the ocean.

To include small, overlooked creatures in his tours, Jan set up some 'touch tanks' on the pier near his boat. Water from the ocean circulated through these large tanks, providing a near perfect replica of ocean conditions. Jan placed several small creatures like clams, anemones and starfish into the tanks to use in his education programs and to share with any curious passersby.

"One day I saw this fellow, a local, walking down the road towards the tanks, doing his best to pretend he wasn't looking at the tanks," Jan remembers. "He was a fairly skeptical sort so I wasn't surprised that he hadn't embraced my tour idea."

But the next evening... "He came along with his wife, and a week later he brought his grandchildren to show them the creatures in the tank," Jan says. "A couple of weeks later he was bringing me some creatures to display in the tank, and within a month he was so excited by the wonders displayed in the tanks that he was hanging around the pier and explaining the contents to visitors."

Here was someone who had worked on the sea all his life, and was still excited at the chance to share some of the things he knew with his family and, eventually, complete strangers. "He has been a great ambassador for the company," Jan says.

On the ship, Jan glories in showing people the ocean from a new angle.

"When you look down into the water, it is clear and appears empty," Jan says, "but when you drag a fine mesh net behind the boat, all of a sudden you have a jar full of interesting animals. One time we examined a squid up close, much to the delight of passengers. Squid have a beak that looks like a parrot's, and everyone was able to see this unique feature."

Some of Jan's customers may look a little rough, but nature has a way of bringing out the kid in everyone.

"One day a group of hard-ass bikers rode up to the pier," Jan said. "They had patches and looked pretty tough. It turned out they loved looking at the touch tanks and spent three hours milling about, looking at the sea life."

Jan remembers taking a group of divers out to do some underwater photography deep on the ocean floor. They were a colorful looking group and Jan had a challenge convincing the local church ladies to host a meal for the group. The women were a bit suspicious of the divers, thinking them a bit 'rough'. The women were pleasantly surprised when the divers arrived for dinner bearing gifts of chocolates. The men raved about the meal and insisted the women relax while they cleaned up the kitchen.

The divers showed the ladies some of the pictures they had taken on the ocean floor. Jan said, "The women had lived near the ocean their whole lives, but never knew that anything like that was there!"

When they left, the divers gave the women one of the pictures as a gift.

"I think the women realized that these were nice people even though they were strangers," Jan recalls, "The last time I visited the hall I saw the picture the divers had left was framed and hung."

Tourists continue to have small, but profound, impacts on the people of Petley. With the loss of fishery jobs and families leaving, the ball diamond had fallen into disrepair.

"I had a group of 12 African-American students up for a tour, and they were surprised to see the baseball field looking so neglected," Jan says.

The group then spent some of their holiday time cleaning up the diamond so they could play ball. "People almost drove off the road when they saw these kids moving boulders off the field," Jan remembers. "A couple of weeks later I noticed that some of the local kids were playing baseball. I hadn't seen anyone using that field for a long time before that."

Jan adds, "I want to continue making the ocean accessible to people and to help them see things they may not otherwise see. I've convinced a researcher from the Department of Fisheries and Oceans to bring an undersea vessel with a camera on a tether here next month. That will let people look at the ocean two hundred metres down."

That is a view that most people will not forget, and will be another way Coastal Connections continues to connect with tourists and its host community.

Preserving The Faroe Islands

"It is not down in any map; true places never are." ~ Herman Melville

"You're number one!" I said.

The Faroe Islands had been voted the Number One ecotourism island destination by National Geographic Traveler and I was speaking to tourism professionals and politicians at their first-ever ecotourism conference.

"This is like winning a tourism Oscar," I explained to the journalist covering the event for a local paper.

"What does this mean for my country?" he asked.

I said, "You will have many people wanting to visit your country now, and it can be a wonderful opportunity if the impacts are properly managed."

The Faroe Islands are a group of eighteen small islands in the Atlantic Ocean about half way between Iceland and Denmark. It is a self-governing region of Denmark and has its own parliament and flag. The Faroese speak their own language, a version of Old Norse, issue their own currency and have the distinction of being one of the world's smallest countries.

You can drive from one end to the other of the biggest island in a few hours in good weather, and there are less than 50,000 people who can claim to be Faroese citizens. Historically, the Faroe residents made their living from fishing and farming; the ubiquitous sheep can be seen on almost every steep grassy cliff.

The architecture, however, is centuries ahead of its time. Green roofs, planted with grass, touted as an environmentally-friendly building technique, are starting to appear in North American cities. The Faroese grass roof is a tradition that goes back hundreds of years; and, while many newer buildings sport tin or tile roofs, there are still many grass roofs. Locals swear the grass roofs are quiet and well insulated.

Will more tourism be good for the Faroe Islands? I knew visitors will be fascinated by this country, far off the beaten path; but one does not just drop in to the Faroe Islands. You have to be determined to visit; but, for people interested in exploring travel frontiers, this idyllic place could prove irresistible.

From North America, it is a two day marathon of connecting flights through Reykjavik or Copenhagen to reach the Faroes. The airport is plagued by frequent fog in the summer, making it difficult for the single airline to stick to flight schedules. Northern Europeans can get there faster by taking the ferry from Copenhagen.

Historically, this place was known as the Land of Maybe – maybe the weather would be good enough to sail or fly and maybe it wouldn't. The Faroe Islands northerly location in the Atlantic and the influence of maritime currents and air masses mean weather is always changing, sometimes dramatically.

People who make the trip will be rewarded with views of the steepest cliffs in Europe and hundreds of thousands of nesting seabirds. You can drive through the Faroe Islands, literally. The Faroese have carved miles of road tunnels through the steep mountains, and in several places, have burrowed under the sea, replacing ferry routes with car tunnels.

The isolation of the Islands supports a vibrant culture. The music coming out the Faroes currently is some of the hottest in Europe, and the fashionable clothing items made from Faroese wool are in demand by trendsetters in New York and London.

My visit to the Faroes was brief and it left me wondering. Government representatives and business owners are thinking hard about their future. They want the opportunities that more tourists would bring, but not at any price. They want to be ready for the new travellers with legislation that will protect the fragile environments and the birds that nest there.

It was reassuring to hear government policy makers discussing tourism caution and not just an unbridled eagerness to increase revenues. As Jan found in the small Newfoundland town of Petley, tourism can have positive impacts on small communities, but it needs to be well-managed and appropriate scale.

I hope that the charm and friendliness that I experienced in the Faroe Islands would remain for other people to enjoy. I know it will be difficult if large numbers of tourists show up on their shores. Fortunately, the Faroese are asking the right questions; and the passion I saw them display as they debated the answers, suggested they were on the right track.

Between A Croc And A Hard Place

"We now no longer camp as for a night, but have settled down on earth and forgotten heaven." ~ Henry David Thoreau

Travel was the motivator behind my career change from accounting to tourism planning, and I have met many other tourism professionals who entered the field as a result of a travel experience. Miles Phillips, coordinator of the nature tourism programs for Agrilife Extension at Texas A&M University, is one.

Miles is a keen advocate for nature and wildlife-based tourism. He helps rural communities develop their infrastructure and services to attract more tourists. He does some guiding and even created a nature photography scavenger hunt game to capitalize on travellers' interest in digital photography.

Miles, like many of the people now working in the tourism industry, did not jump into the field right after university. He was working as an engineer when a chance travel experience sparked a career switch.

When Mile's grandfather passed away in 1994, at the grand old age of 100, Mile's parents decided to take their share of the inheritance and treat their family to an African safari. Before long a trip was booked to Namibia and Zimbabwe.

"We were always a wildlife family," Miles remembers. "My dad is a wildlife biologist and my brothers and I would go hunting every fall."

The chance to see African wildlife in its native habitat was something everyone was looking forward to, but the unexpected highlight for Miles was observing the game guides in action.

"Their ability to share detailed information made the whole trip," Miles said.

The game guides led Miles and his family on a kayak trip, on walks through the bush and on game drives. They opened Miles' eyes to a new way of seeing the world.

"I remember watching how they read animal tracks; and one day, an old guide stuck his finger right in the elephant poop to see how fresh it was!" Miles said, "They didn't even need to see an animal to identify it. They could distinguish one from another just by seeing the gleam of their eyes at night."

"We camped out in the Namib Desert under the stars and in the morning found Oryx tracks within ten feet of where we had been sleeping," he said. "We drove along the Skeleton Coast without seeing another human for the entire day. I even managed to get a great souvenir poster of a game guide leading a hunting safari." Africa was growing on Miles, and he wanted to experience more of its magic.

Later, Miles and his brothers signed up for a whitewater rafting trip on the famed Zambezi River. This is one of the most challenging of whitewater rafting experiences with class five and six rapids and, when Miles visited, unexploded land mines from the civil war could still be found along the banks.

"Our guide was an ex-special forces officer," Miles said, "The day included the thrilling experience of flipping the raft and climbing back in, careful of course to avoid the crocodiles in the river and any land mines on the banks!"

Miles' mom was having a different type of experience off the river. Her nose had started to bleed and it went on for several hours with no sign of stopping. As a nurse, she knew it was important to get treatment, so the group headed for Victoria Falls hospital.

Surprised at how little the hospital staff had to work with, Miles' mother emptied her suitcase of the medications she had brought and gave them to the hospital. Her donation would help the staff deal with some of their less-serious cases; but she had to be airlifted to the capital, Harare, for surgery.

Then came a real surprise. Miles discovered the surgeon in the hospital was the guide featured on the poster he had collected in Namibia. The guide/doctor had made a dramatic career change and Miles started thinking that maybe he could as well.

"When I got back home after the trip, the role of a guide and all the great guides I'd seen in action stayed with me," Miles said, "Eventually I made a career change into the field of ecotourism and I am happy I did."

Very Much Trouble

"Those that say you can't take it with you never saw a car packed for a vacation trip." ~ Author Unknown

Take too much luggage when you travel and you will find yourself on the wrong end of an excess weight charge and the scowl of an airline employee. Brian Keating, Head of Conservation Outreach, for the Calgary Zoo, managed to get in Very Much Trouble with some of the world's most unusual luggage on Air Zimbabwe.

As part of his job, Brian has been leading trips to the world's best wildlife watching destinations for decades. In the mid 1980s he came across a perfect elephant skull specimen in a Zimbabwe national park warehouse. The bull had been about forty when he had been shot.

"He hadn't been poached," Brian remembers, "The front of his face would have been chopped up (to remove the ivory), and this skull was in excellent shape." He decided the skull would be a valuable addition to the Zoo's bio-fact collection and education programs. The park officials concurred, so Brian started the laborious process of getting it to Canada.

Because elephants are an endangered species transporting the skull would require permits from both the Canadian and Zimbabwe governments. Brian was able to get the Canadian permits quickly, but the African paperwork bogged down. For five years, Brian wrote letters and met with government officials when he travelled to Zimbabwe. The doorman at Harare's Monomatapa Hotel, well aware of Brian's labours, dubbed the skull, 'Mningeedouwa'. "Mr. Keating, it means very much trouble," he chuckled, something Brian agreed with.

Finally, Brian had his export permit. He also got a letter from the head of Air Zimbabwe waiving any baggage charges. "It would have cost hundreds of dollars in overweight charges if the skull had been treated like regular luggage," Brian said.

Anticipating an uneasy passage, Brian dressed in his best safari jacket and slacks, and asked his driver to don a suit before they headed to the crowded airport.

"In African fashion, if one person is travelling, 30 more show up to see them off," Brian remembers. Not wanting to stand in line with the skull, Brian had a better strategy.

"Follow me," Brian told the driver. They picked up the three foot skull, balancing the hundred plus pounds between them. Brian proceeded to say "excuse me" as they walked into the airport and past the people lined up.

"I just kept saying 'excuse me' and people let us pass," he said. "We walked to the front of the line, and I kept saying 'excuse me.' We got to the check-in counter, and the weigh scale in the opening between ticket wickets. I said 'excuse me' and we stepped over the scale and walked behind the counter.

"I spotted the luggage conveyor belt and a door next to it. We carried the elephant over to the door, said 'excuse me' to the guard wielding a machine gun, and walked onto the tarmac. I spotted our plane being loaded in the early evening air. I kept saying 'excuse me,' and since we looked very official, no one stopped us. We excused ourselves all the way to the plane and into the cargo hold.

"We placed the skull in the belly of the plane and I said good-bye to my driver," Brian remembers. "I went back into the airport and took my place beside my wife, Dee, in the lineup. We got our boarding passes, walked on the plane and settled in. I relaxed, knowing I had finally got the elephant skull and it was on its way to Canada," Brian said.

But....

"Ahead of us, a short confused-looking East-Indian woman was dragging several carry-on bags. She had a seat in the emergency exit row which has no overhead bins. Looking for storage, she reached over and pulled the emergency door exit handle," Brian recounts. Immediately the CO_2 canisters blasted the door out of the way and the emergency slide unfolded and inflated. "There was noise and mayhem everywhere," Brian said.

President Robert Mugabe and several of his cabinet ministers were sitting in first class when the door blew. A long row of limousines pulled up to the plane and the officials were evacuated quickly. "It was like peas being spit out of a pea shooter," Brian said. "When a towering steward approached the tiny woman, she opted for the 'admit nothing' strategy. 'I just touched it, I just touched it,' she said over and over again.

Repacking the emergency chute and the life rafts would take time so Air Zimbabwe sent the passengers to a hotel, telling them to come back the next day. After a night's rest, Brian and Dee returned and lined up with the other passengers on the tarmac.

Brian said, "In those days you had to physically point to your luggage before it was loaded on the plane. I saw all these suitcases lined up, but there was no Mningeedouwa! I was afraid he had been stolen, but I went to the airplane and looked in the hold. There, in the dark belly of the airplane, I could just make out the skull of Mningeedouwa – Very Much Trouble. He was safe and ready for the trip to Canada. I swear he winked at me!"

"And to this day, Dee and I use the expression 'I just touched it, I just touched it' whenever something goes wrong on our trips."

(Almost) Climbing Mt. Kinabalu

"Wherever you go, there you are." ~ Jon Kabat-Zinn

Sometimes the changes that travel makes in our lives are not the result of successes. When I took on Borneo's Mt. Kinabalu, I discovered that not getting the experience I was seeking can be just as worthwhile as having everything going according to plan.

At 4,095 metres, about 13,500 feet, Mt. Kinabalu is the tallest mountain in Southeast Asia. Climbing this mountain is a popular activity with adventure travellers visiting Malaysia. It can be done in two days by most people of reasonable fitness levels; or in the absence of good fitness, with a whole lot of determination.

I had heard people talk about climbing Mt. Kinabalu when I first visited Borneo in 2001. A 70-year-old woman, attending the Asia Pacific Ecotourism Conference I was speaking at, had summited the mountain the day prior to the conference launch. She received a round of enthusiastic applause for her accomplishment from the attendees. There were pictures flashed on the auditorium screen showing the beauty of this mountain peak and I thought to myself that, one day, climbing the mountain would be a cool thing to do. I got my wish a few years later when I went back to Borneo to speak again. I made arrangements to stay after the conference for a few days to attempt the mountain climb.

I was amused to find out that because I was a regular hiker of the Rocky Mountains near my home, I was scheduled to hike the longer and more arduous route up Mt. Kinabalu. It was a less crowded trek with a greater chance to see unique and changing vegetation along the trail.

I was a bit uneasy about the planned route, but I figured if I hiked slowly enough I should be able to make the top. The normal chain of events for hikers is to arrive at Mt. Kinabalu National Park the evening before the hike to register. Early the next morning the hike starts after a hearty breakfast. The goal is to reach the Lodge and the primitive cabins perched at 11,000 feet by the afternoon of the first day.

Supper is provided and everyone catches a few hours of sleep before starting out for the summit at 2 a.m. in the hope of reaching the top at sunrise, and then hiking back down the same day. I guess it's one of those things that reads so well in travel brochures, but feels a whole lot different when you are actually living it.

As my shuttle van dropped me at the park office to register, my escort cheerfully informed me she had saved me some money by canceling the porter who would carry my bag. The $20US porter fee would not have caused me any financial stress; but the thought of carrying all my gear up the mountain peak myself almost gave me a coronary. I was having trouble seeing the top of the mountain even with my head tipped all the way back. It was going to take more than the old backpacking trick of sawing my toothbrush in half to save weight, to survive this trip.

The morning of the hike dawned sunny and clear with no rain forecast; something that is not common and for which I was profoundly grateful. As a visiting tourism expert, I was to have my own guide, Raoul, and the chance to learn more about this very special mountain.

Raoul probably found me a bit pushy. We had barely exchanged names and I was eager to reopen negotiations on carrying my pack. Fortunately, Raoul was a good sport as well as a fit man for he agreed to carry my pack leaving me with just my camera and day's food to pack.

Within minutes of setting out, I knew this was going to be a hike I would never forget. The trail was extremely steep; initially it was steep uphill, and then it was steep downhill as we followed the undulating trail through the rainforest. In my own hiking experience, steep hills can be conquered by taking small steps and walking slowly. Like finding out you have been studying physics for a biology exam, I realized hiking techniques for the Rockies were the wrong kind of preparation for hiking in Borneo.

The roots of the huge trees lining the trails crisscrossed the path; their giant buttresses created a type of stairway up the mountain. Instead of taking little steps and walking up the slope, each hiker was forced to step up over the roots. It was like a giant staircase; and, unlike the song Stairway to Heaven, it became the stairway to hell in short order. My quadriceps muscles screamed with the effort of stepping up these large steps, time and time again. We would rest frequently, but I could never seem to recover. The rapid increase in elevation was starving my cells of oxygen, and they were unable to repair themselves with the short rests.

We had been hiking a couple of hours when we started to encounter the people who had summitted that morning, and were now descending. Many of them bounded by us with an almost fanatical gleam in their eye that seemed to say they had taken on the world and come out the victor. Others were not doing as well.

One particular group of hikers was resting beside the trail when we came upon them. Resting is the polite word; in reality they were laying half off the trail writhing in agony. Their faces were twisted in grimaces and they were massaging their legs in a futile effort to relieve the pain. Raoul and the other guide spoke a few words in their native tongue and we carried on.

I asked what they had been discussing. Raoul said the other guide had told him that he thought it would be almost midnight before the group would get off the mountain. It was only mid-morning! It was a vivid reminder that getting off the mountain would be almost as hard as climbing it; one would need to save some energy for the return trip.

As the hike progressed, I found it harder and harder. The trail never seemed to get any easier, and my leg muscles ached constantly. To take my mind off my spaghetti-like legs I started to entertain my mind with any distraction I could come up with. I tried to figure out how many hikers looked to be my age or older. I stopped that one pretty fast when I realized there were not many. My morale started to slip.

———————————

I searched for people that were limping along, er, climbing, at my pace and tried to strike up conversations. I met some great people, but small talk is challenging when you are gasping for air like a goldfish at feeding time. Soon I gave up any attempt at conversation.

With about six hours of climbing behind me, I was despairing of even reaching the Lodge, never mind the summit; but I was determined. I was also afraid of humiliating myself by having to turn around. My guide could tell I was feeling rough and in his limited English told me stories of his family. I could see even he was finding the going rough and felt guilty that he was carrying my pack as well as trying to keep up my morale.

I have always been what is politely described as task-orientated, but I was starting to realize that I might not be able to make the summit. Or a more accurate description of the situation might be that I was not sure I wanted to make the effort needed to make the summit. I couldn't see myself, in Chariots of Fire fashion, crawling up to the summit, and then repeating the descent drama we had seen earlier in the day. I loved Borneo, but I had no desire to see the inside of one of its hospitals.

Judging by the number of people on the trail, one less summiteer would not be noticed so I had to ask myself why I wanted to finish. Would it be such a bad thing if I quit when I reached the Lodge? For me this was a huge drama in my mind. I was used to success, and I believed you could accomplish anything if you put your mind to it. I guess if my life had depended upon it, I could have reached the summit; but it didn't and I felt it was more important to enjoy the rest of the time in Borneo. I was more eager to get my food from room service than from a hospital orderly.

I finally told my guide I was going to stop at the Lodge and hike back the next morning without trying for the summit. I am sure he thought his ears were failing him. "I feel sad for you," he said. I was sad too, but I had to make the best decision I could. Perhaps I was being too cautious, but when I rolled out of bed at 2 a.m. to bid my cabin mates good luck on their climb, I was sure I had made the right decision.

I am nervous about heights and my legs were still not talking to me, so the idea of not having to climb another two thousand feet in the dark with weary muscles had me doing a little victory dance as I wandered back into the cabin for another few hours of shut eye.

Shortly after dawn, I got up for a good breakfast and started down the trail with Raoul. We had the trail almost to ourselves as the people going to the summit had not yet reached us on their downward descent, and the people starting their odyssey that day had not climbed that far. Without the pressure of wondering whether I was going to survive the trip (I was pretty sure I would now), I was able to enjoy the views and the vegetation.

We encountered several porters carrying all manner of stuff up the trail: large boxes, timbers for construction projects, even a large door! Their efforts made the struggles of the tourists seem meager in comparison. As we came to one busy part of the trail, I heard someone call out "It's Carol Patterson!" Like most people, I am probably more famous in my own mind than in that of others, so I was a little surprised to be flagged down on a remote mountain trail in Borneo.

The person who had recognized me turned out to be someone who had heard me speaking at the conference and was returning to his job at the Lodge high up the mountain. Talk about your long walks to work!

We chatted for a few minutes and I realized that I was far more moved by the fact that my words had made an impression on this hard-working tourism manager, than whether or not I had conquered the mountain. In that few minutes, it became abundantly clear to me that the journey is the destination.

Epilogue

"I love to travel, but hate to arrive." ~ Albert Einstein

As I reflect on my travels and listen to other tourists' tales, the temptation to hit the road is stronger. I realize that I find the best part of me while travelling. Yes, I'm scared witless at times, but as my Arctic-exploring friend, Keith Dewing, points out, travel makes us more honest with ourselves. I think it also brings out the best in us. When I'm inches from a grey whale as it slips beneath the ocean's surface, I'm immersed in the moment. I'm not worried about some inane technology created by mankind to supposedly improve our world, but that makes mine more stress-filled. All I can think about is the perfection created by Mother Nature and I am humbled by the grace and beauty her creatures display.

Travel lifts us out of our comfort zone and lets us use skills developed from hard knocks and training. It also brings us face to face with our inner being, and while we may be surprised at the introduction, we find we're ready for challenges coming our way. Wandering out of our daily routine means we try new things and we see how others regard the world. Sometimes we're smug in our normalcy, especially as compared to our travelling companions; other times we have much to learn.

All travel creates an inner adventure allowing us to reinvent ourselves over and over again. There is no age limit or skill requirement for Reinventure; it is merely the willingness to open our eyes and hearts to possible change. Pick a destination or an activity you want to experience and figure out how to get there. If your budget is small, your trips may be shorter or closer to home, or you may need to combine work with travel; but there is always a way.

I've gathered some of my favorite travel places and companies on my website www.reinventuretravel.com. Check it out for some ideas to start your Reinventure process.

May all your adventures be engaging and fruitful! I hope you discover the outer beauty to be found in nature and the inner beauty that travel can reveal.

Carol

Index

Reinventure

Know Someone Who Needs A Reinventure?

Help Your Loved Ones, Friends and Colleagues
Discover the Reinventure Possibilities of Travel

Check Your Local Bookstore Or Order Here

For credit card or International orders, please call
1-800-232-4444 or visit www.trafford.com

For direct orders, please send me _____ copies of
Reinventure: How Travel Can Change Your Life

Canadian Orders	**U.S. Orders**
For each copy, send a Money Order for $25.94 ($18.99 + 95¢ GST + $6 S&H)	For each copy, send a Postal Money Order for $28.99 ($18.99 + $10 S&H)

Money order for $_____ is enclosed.

Name:
Organization:
Mailing Address:
City/Province or State/ Postal Code or ZIP:
Phone: _____ _____ _____ Email: _____

Mail to:
Kalahari Management Inc.
PO Box 46056, Inglewood RPO
Calgary, Alberta, Canada T2G 5H7

Email: info@kalahari-online.com

Visit our website for more information on
Reinventures and meaningful travel
www.reinventuretravel.com

Author is available for speaking engagements

160

ISBN 1425169791-1

9 781425 169794